THE

HUGUENOT LOVERS.

A TALE OF THE OLD DOMINION.

BY

C. P. E. BURGWYN,

A. B., C. E., M. AM. SOC. C. E.,

Assistant Engineer in local charge of the Improvement of the
James River; Consulting Engineer Lee Monument Asso-
ciation; Consulting Engineer Hollywood Ceme-
tery Company; Principal Virginia
Mechanics Institute
(Night School of Technology).

RICHMOND, VA.:

PUBLISHED BY THE AUTHOR.

1889.

PRESS OF BAUGHMAN BROTHERS,
RICHMOND, VA.

TO
THE MEMORY OF THOSE OF MY PEOPLE WHO HAVE
SUNK TO THEIR ETERNAL REST WHEN OBEY-
ING THEIR COUNTRY'S LAWS, THIS
CREATION IS DEDICATED.

PREFACE.

In the autumn of 1888 the Author was engaged in assisting at the transferring of the Monitor fleet from City Point to an anchorage near Richmond, Va. After the heavy vessels were under way, there was an interval of several hours each day, in which he had no duties to perform, and it was during this brief respite from the demands of a busy professional career that most of these pages were written.

The Author offers to the critical public this explanation of the circumstance of the writing, in order that they may find excuse for a possible abruptness in some of its parts. He also asks indulgence for his effort at portraiture of the characteristic of devotedness in the negro. If an excuse is needed for this, he trusts that it will be found in his desire to put upon record, so as to be remembered whenever this book is read, the act of one of that race who protected the dead body of his brother on the battle-field of Gettysburg.

THE HUGUENOT LOVERS.

CHAPTER I.

THE JOURNEY.

It was on a cold bleak day in the early part of March, when the northwest wind had blown for several days until it seemed as if the life would be frozen from out of every animate thing, that a young girl sat in the bay-window of a comfortable house on Beacon street, in Boston.

She had just come in from an outdoor walk, enforced by her great love for the pure air, and was sitting in the sunshine of a dying winter day, endeavoring to draw from Nature, some of the vivifying effects of the glorious sun-rays.

The cold damp air had benumbed her sensibilities, and she was slowly recovering her animation from the

artificial warmth of a steam-heated
room. The prospect before her indeed was glorious. There had been
a sleet, and all the trees of the Com-
mon and Public Garden, were covered
with icicles and tiny particles of ice,
which, forming prismatic colors, lit
up the landscape with a thousand
hues. There was the Charles river,
lashed into fury by the howling wind,
and as the waves struck the various
piers, a spray of foam was dashed
over their surfaces, which, quickly
congealing into new icicles, added to
the brilliancy of the refraction. It
was indeed a beautiful sight—but all
was cold. Shuddering, the young
girl turned from the scene; for while
the coloring and brilliant appearance
of the landscape, was sufficient to
satisfy the ideal of the wildest artist,
yet there was a coldness about it all
which she well knew was a concomi-
tant of death. Heat is life, but cold

is death, and when her sympathetic
nature realized how much suffering
was being undergone by women less
fortunately housed than herself, she
was filled with a sadness such as was
felt by Guatama, when, abandoning
His ethereal home, He set out on the
redemption of a suffering world. She
was a girl of scarce twenty years, of
Boston's bluest blood, and of direct
descent from the Pilgrim Fathers.

Her father was a man of considerable means, and having decided lite-
rary tastes, had spent his life in such
pursuits. An early fondness for historical researches had turned his attention to subjects connected with
the middle ages and times cotempo-
rary with the early settlement of this
country. Of the great events of this
century, particularly of that part re-
lating to the great war between the
States, he knew but little, and he
passed through those stirring times

without realizing that History **was**
being made before his very eyes while
he was delving into the manufactured
history of a past era. Of late he was
beginning to realize this   He was beginning to sum up his life-work, and
though he would endeavor to shut
out the thought, yet the conclusion
would sometimes come to him un-
awares, that, as far as his talent was
concerned, it had been buried. Possessed of decided wealth, even in that
city of millionaires, he had turned
over his property to trusty lawyers,
and they having invested it with that
sagacity and skill which has been the
great characteristic of its legal frater-
nity, he had no thought save of his
income. This being large, he had
saved up much of it, and thus being
free from the anxieties of a struggle
for existence, he had devoted himself
to his favorite pursuits and studies.
But when he thought of how little he

had done in this world, how little he had added to its knowledge, or how little he had ameliorated the condition of mankind, the conclusion was being forced upon him that future generations could not rise up and call blessings upon him—that the world was not better because he had lived; and, being the last of his race, with only this one daughter, he felt at last that he had *lived* and *lost*. It is true that he had written a book or two, but these he had published at his own expense, and after having been glanced over by some of his friends, and, worse than all, praised only by those whom he knew were sycophants, had dropped into oblivion. These experiments were the subject of much jest by his intimate friends.

He had travelled much, and it was with great pride that he saw how his native country had surpassed the other nations of the world. He had

looked down from the top of the
Great Pyramid of Egypt and had admired its colossal proportions, but he
had seen the Great Bridge over the
East river, and he knew that beside
it the Great Pyramid was as nothing.
The one was the epitome of brute
strength, the other the creation of
intelligent science. He had loved to
read of Rameses, of Cyrus, and of the
great leaders of antiquity, but he realized that before the Gatling guns,
and rifles of American invention, the
armies of the Old World would have
been blotted from existence like the
trees of a forest before a tropical hur-
ricane. He had read of the forced
marches of Xenophon and Alexander,
yet he had travelled on the American
continent in a magnificently furnished
car, and had dined sumptuously while
so doing. He had traversed in a few
hours a distance greater than the far-
thest expeditions of the most famous

monarchs of ancient history. He was
beginning to take in the fact that posterity will point to our epoch as one
of the greatest that has yet appeared
upon the globe· yet what had he done
towards helping it on? He had not
grown two blades of grass where one
was growing before. As old age was
advancing upon him this consciousness increased. Noi did he have a son
upon whom to transfer the mantle of
his garment. Upon his daughter, and
to her alone, must descend the heritage
of many ancestors. Therefore he had
lavished upon her all the affectionate
care and solicitude of his life. Her
education had been a great source of
anxiety to him. Yet in this respect
he had done himself credit. He had
had her under the charge of the most
distinguished teacher of that most
distinguished city of literati, and, as
far as book knowledge was concerned,
he had done his best. She had accom-

panied him on his last travels in Europe, and had therefore seen something, as he thought, of life.

He had lost his wife when his daughter was quite a child, and therefore the management of his household had descended upon her when she was yet young in years; hence, as regards housekeeping, she had ample experience. He himself was rather delicate in constitution, but had married the daughter of an old-time New England farmer. His wife was possessed of the physical strength and beauty that can only accrue to those of active out-door pursuits. From her mother the daughter had inherited that beauty of limb and grace of person that so distinguished her. From her father she inherited her patrician face.

Such was Edyth Prescott, as she sat in that sun lighted window of that wintry afternoon. Would that pen

of mine could convey a just conception of the fair young girl as she sat
that afternoon in a pensive attitude,
thinking on the great problem of life.
The aristocratic face, usually so eager-
looking, with its pair of brilliant ha-
zel eyes, and ruddy cheeks, was now
wrapt in contemplation, saddened, as
it appeared, by a passing thought,
such as a painter might evoke of the
young musician when trying to recall
the lost chord which had sounded its
grand amen.

Of late years, unconsciously to herself, her form had developed into a
symmetry which was surpassingly
beautiful to behold, and the careful
training she had undergone had
rounded her limbs to that extent
which the Latin poet has so charm-
ingly described as wholly perfection.
Her chest was broad, while her bosom
rose and fell with each inhalation of
the air, as can only be done by those

of well-developed proportions.   Her
hair was of that color which has ever
been the artist's dream—which it took
a Titian to perpetuate in ideal form.
Such color of hair is always accompanied by fairness of skin, and
in truth her neck and bosom were
of such structure that once, having
occasion for leaving a ball-room to
go to an open conservatory, a youthful admirer had applied to her, with
all the enthusiasm of his youth, the
language of that poet who said—

> The envious snow came down in haste
>   To prove thy breast less fair;
> But grieved to find itself surpassed,
>   It melts into a tear.

The brilliancy of coloring in her
cheeks had been the theme of many
an admirer's song, but her careful
father had feared that it was the one
outward and visible sign of the only
imperfection in her nature.   She was
open-handed and generous, and at

times the warm blood flowed to and
from her heart in such volume as to
overload it. The subtle action of her
heart had been a source of danger to
her, but the knowledge of this fact
had been withheld. Perhaps it was
to this overflow of her heart that her
generous nature was due. She was
above suspicion and beyond deceit.
A nobler disposition never drew its
inspiration from an animate form.
Such is but a vain attempt to portray the character of the girl as it
was about to be developed by the
succeeding events.

She had many admirers. Her first
idea of life, colored somewhat from her
father's pursuits, was to be the help-
mate of some college professor. In
aiding and encouraging him she hoped
to find a field for that talent she felt
that she possessed. With this idea in
mind she had attended many of the
assemblies of the students at Cam-

bridge. Her disappointment was
great. Those who were the most
agreeable, and were of a disposition
akin to her own, were as a general thing wretchedly poor scholars.
Those who were of high scholastic
standing were either her inferiors in
social standing, or else were wanting
in those refined and delicate feelings
and manners which are essential to a
highly-cultivated woman in the man
she loves.

This first idea being thus ruthlessly
overthrown, her next feeling was that
she would do good in the world by
being the patron of some charitable
or religious institution; that she
would eschew society and devote herself to these and kindred occupations.
With this idea in view she sat in her
comfortable apartment, revolving in
her mind what was the best prac-
tical manner of making some com-
mencement upon this plan, when her

father entered and interrupted her in the midst of her meditations.

He noticed with concern the brilliant color and pensive attitude, and quietly resolved that he would take more care of her than ever before. A brightening of the countenance and a look of consciousness came into her eyes as she greeted her father—a look which revealed the soul that was within her eyes; for there is no one thing on earth which so manifests the spirit that is within us as the intelligence that our eyes reveal.

"Good afternoon, my child. What is it that is so engaging your attention as to make your expression resemble that of the captive Andromache?" was the greeting that startled her in her reverie, and brought her suddenly back to worldly things.

"Nothing, papa; I was only thinking how I could be of some use to somebody, and not to pass my time so idly and unprofitably."

Now, if there was one thing above all others which Mr. Prescott detested, it was a woman's-rights woman, in the so-called political sense of the word. He feared that his daughter would become what was characterized in Boston as "strong-minded," and thus lose that gentleness of demeanor which was her inexpressible charm. He therefore silently resolved to separate Edyth from such possible influences, and as he had been conversing with his sister upon the subject, and had secured her consent to accompany him with her daughter, he decided that the best way to do this was by taking a trip to the South and having Edyth accompany him.

A trip to the sunny South! Who is there, who, living in the frozen North, and at a time when everything is cold and dead, but that would be glad of the opportunity of visiting that section of country, of which so much has been said and sung? How can pen of mine do justice to that region for which Nature has done so much? How can its glorious climate best be described, or how can the beauty of its women and valor of its men be depicted best?

To tell the truth, Mr. Prescott had thought very little of its people. He had thought most of its climate. As a young man, to him it had been the home of slavery, and, being an abolitionist himself, he was ready to believe the gross inaccuracies and misconceptions that had existed concerning it.

During the period of the great war it had been to him as an ultima thule, and the men who had sacrificed their fortunes and their lives were, in his estimation, merely rebels and overthrowers of good government. Since the war he had regarded its people as

conspirators, members of secret or-
ganizations or leagues, and ready, as
a solid phalanx, to turn upon all who
visited their domain.

He had a sort of admiration, founded on military enthusiasm, for the man
who, "standing like a stone wall,"
had defeated an army that was considered irresistible, and the character
of the Great Chieftain who, after laying down his sword, took up the
book, in order to instruct the coming
generation, had appealed powerfully
to his sensibilities; but men of this
stamp he had considered as either
killed during the war or else dead
long ago, and that the country was
now inhabited by persons of entirely
a different character—repudiators of
their just debts, braggadocios, and
otherwise undesirable as acquaintances.

To Edyth the men of the South
were as cow-boys—personally brave

enough, but wanting in all that re-
finement and delicacy of feeling so
essential in what she termed a gentleman. To her the women were as of
gaudy appearance and thriftless in
their habits, and altogether uncon-
genial.

.With such opinions,when her father
asked her how she would like a trip
to the South, she acquiesced without
much anticipation of any pleasure,
only to conform to her father's incli-
nations, and to gratify him by her
ready desire to agree with him in his
plans. Accordingly, therefore, it was
agreed upon that they should start
for Richmond the next evening, stopping at Washington on their way,
and after being joined by her aunt
and cousin, to continue their travels
where time and chance might determine.

The next evening witnessed her
father and herself comfortably estab-

lished on the New York and New
England train, and although it continued bitterly cold, and the wind
kept blowing a gale, yet the appli-
ances of the parlor-car were such that
they experienced but little of the out-
door rigors.

The next morning Edyth aroused
early, so as to avoid the unpleasant-
ness of dressing in a sleeping-car before others, and, having arranged her
toilet, came out upon the platform
just as the transfer was being made
around the city of New York.   The
first object which met her gaze was
the East River Bridge.   Coated with
ice, it reflected the rays of the rising
sun, and broke them up into millions
of colors.   But it was not the beauty
of the bridge that elicited her admiration.   It was the thought of the
men who had designed the plan and
had constructed it that awoke a responsive chord in her feelings. Father

and son, she had heard, had done it;
and how glorious it must have been
for them to have worked in such har-
monious relationship. Oh! that she
could have been connected with it
in some way, and that her name
should go down to posterity linked
with the memory of the builders
of this structure, besides which the
mighty efforts of the Pharaohs were
as nothing, and compared to which
the loftiest edifices of Greece and
Rome were pigmean. Compared to
this, the temple of the Byzantine Em-
peror was insignificant, and the Rock
of St. Peter itself, although the product of four centuries of builders,
was liliputian. Here the hand of
father and son alone, in the short
space of a lifetime, had erected a
structure which far surpassed anything the world had previously beheld. Here the designer, after being
injured upon his work, bed-ridden,

watched its progress from his window
by a telescopic vision, and with his
drawings and his models carried it to
completion.   Here had been no lash
of taskmaster or labor of captives
taken in war.   It was the product of
American skill and ingenuity, backed
by American combination of capital.

With such thoughts as these awa-
kened in her mind, she was prepared
somewhat to take in, during the short
stop in Philadelphia, the magnificent
proportions of its famous hall.   Here
again, was an example of what had
been done for the benefit of the future,
as well as of the present, generation.
This building, marvellous in itself,
was made a hundred-fold more so in
her estimation when she reflected that
it had been constructed in the short
space of sixteen years, and by the
citizens of a single American city,
which had hardly had much more than
two centuries of municipal existence.

Cyrus had built his palaces after he had the combined strength of the Medes and Persians to assist him; Alexander, after conquering the world, had found life too short to do more than name a city. The Great Peter, with North-eastern Europe, and Northern Asia, had done nothing which could be compared to this, and the Grand Monarch of France had not equalled it in his structures. But the time consumed at the railroad station was too short to admit of many reflections like these, and, after taking a hasty glance at the building, she was compelled to return to the train to resume her southward flight; and, while traversing the country at a speed which the ancients would have regarded as miraculous, she reflected how curious it was that she had gone over many buildings in Europe, and had been astonished at them, while here in her own country, was a building which surpassed

them all—of which she had never
even heard, much less seen, for, to her
shame must it be confessed, that having imbibed the prejudices of New
England, she had deemed that all
that was worth seeing in this country
was either in Boston or New York,
and that if one wanted to see the
great structures of the world they
must go abroad to do it. If she had
ever heard of the great building in
Philadelphia, she had forgotten it;
certainly she had no previous conception of its magnificence.

When the train was approaching
Baltimore she was unable to see much
of that city, and for some time her
impressions of it were of a city of
tunnels and smoke, and generally disagreeable. The sun had now come
out, the wind had lulled, and she became conscious of a great change in
the outside temperature when she
went on the platform of the car.

Her first impression of Washington

was curious. A long way off she saw the dome of the Capitol, appearing to equal in height the obelisk to Washington. This she knew was not the fact, inasmuch as it was well known that the Washington monument was the highest structure that had yet been built by human means; and she did not comprehend that the eminence of the position of the Capitol and the point of view made the perspective as she saw it. It was while trying to reconcile these ideas that the train hurried her into the city before she had time to realize it all, and the great change in curvature in coming into the depot having escaped her attention, she beheld, after arrival, the monument on her left hand instead of on her right. By this time it was growing dark. The streets, well illuminated with the powerful electric lights, with their wide dimensions, was so contrary to her expectations

that she became at first confused,
then dazed, and finally lost the reck-
oning of all her surroundings.

It was in this state of mind that
she was not now so much surprised,
when she found that at the hotel, dinner was announced instead of supper,
or when, later in the evening, on accompanying her father to the theatre,
she beheld Washington society in
full-dress attendance at the opera.
The first appearance of the house was
dazzling. To one accustomed to the
sombre hue of the black dress-coat
and constraining air of Boston, the
bright colors of the uniforms of the
officers and costumes of foreign offi-
cials was striking, indeed.

She occupied a seat next to a person who seemed familiar with the appearance of the different spectators,
and who was naming them to a friend,
evidently a stranger. Here was an
Ambassador Extraordinary and Min-

ister Plenipotentiary, with all sorts
of ornaments which in Boston might
have appeared out of place, but which
did not now seem incongruous; there
was an *attache* to the British Lega-
tion, whose figure the brilliant red
uniform set off to great advantage.
A Chinese Mandarin, an Austrian
Hussar, a Turkish Pasha with the
wildest sorts of rumors about his harem, formed but a small part of the
galaxy of those present. It was indeed a pleasing sight to the eye; and
to the ear, the sweet music of an
Italian opera seemed a fitting accom-
paniment to such a scene.

She had classed Washington in her
mind with New Bedford, to which
place she had once been to some private theatricals; but what a difference
was the reality! It seemed to her
like enchantment, and when she retired for the night her mind was filled
with the most confused ideas; she

2

dreamed of courts and camps, of martial men issuing forth to conquer the
world, of being carried off into an
Eastern seraglio and there rescued by
a hero, who, encircling her with the
stars and stripes, threatened destruction with a revolving cannon upon
any who molested her. She awoke
in the morning, prepared to accept
new ideas and impressions. The Bos-
tonian was eliminated; the cosmo-
politan was substituted in its stead.

CHAPTER II.

THE MEETING.

Such was Edyth Prescott, her past history and her present environments, at the opening of the scenes we are now about to describe. How little did she realize that a critical moment was upon her, and that she was about to pass through an epoch in her existence which would dominate all the remainder of her life, and whose effects would go down all succeeding time. None of us appreciate the time at its being, but when it has passed, we look back upon the great crises of our life, and wonder if we could have been the same then as now.

She sat down at the breakfast-table, in maiden meditation, fancy free.

She arose from it with the image of a
man so impressed upon her imagination that all after efforts to eradicate
it were unavailing, and, try as she
might, she felt unable to banish from
her memory the sound of his voice
and the light of his eye. Her father
had stopped down stairs to get the
morning paper, and left her to go
into the dining-room alone. She was
ushered to a small table, and was
waiting there for her father's return,
when, with a gesture and a flourish
such as only a darkey head-waiter or
drum-major can assume, a gentleman
was shown by the waiter to a seat
next to her's. Although she did not
look up, she was conscious of his gaze
being fixed upon her. It is only one
who has been enthralled by the prim-
ness of a puritan's demeanor that can
appreciate the horror almost with
which she saw this man shake hands
with a waiter, and a colored waiter

at that, in this the dining-room of one
of the fashionable hotels in Washington. The words that were said were
novel to her hearing.

"'Fore de Lord, Marse Ran., who
wud ha' tho't dat you wuz hyar; dat
I shud ha' seed you lookin' like dis
when de las' time I seed you you wuz
so bad off!"

"Yes, Tom, I am the same person
that you rescued. But for you I
would have been in a very bad way.
What are you up to now, and is there
anything I can do for you?"

Before Tom had time to reply he
was called away, and as Colonel Randolph Carter turned around it was
with great rapidity that Edyth had
to look away, in order that he might
not see how intently she had been gaz-
ing at him. To cover up her confusion, she appeared to be searching for
some object on the table, and he,
thinking she wanted a spoon, handed
one to her.

This she disdainfully took no notice of, and he, not appearing to perceive this, asked her if there was anything he could hand her.

"If you speak to me again, sir, I will call the head-waiter," was the response of the imperious girl.

With a look of mild surprise he raised his eyes until he looked straight into hers.

To her dying day she never forgot that look. To describe it to herself she often tried; to analyse it she in vain essayed, and afterwards she kept on wondering whether he ever recollected the occurrence. It seemed to her his eye slowly pierced into her very soul. It searched her heart. It read her thought.

Turning away, Col. Carter caught the eye of the head-waiter, and, summoning him, requested that he be given a seat near to the window, in order to see better to read his paper.

He got up without looking at her

again, and as he moved along she
overheard one of the waiters say,
"Bress my sole, I tho't Culn. Carter
wud ha' stuck side a pretty gal like
dat."

Her father joined her then, and she,
feeling safe from any unpleasant en-
counter, began to examine carefully
the man who had caused her this
momentary vexation.

He was not what would be called
a handsome man. Some might even
go so far as to deny him the attribute
of good looks; but there was an undefinable something about his face
which, when closely studied, would
indicate that there was a world of
powerful force behind that apparently
placid reserve. He was a man of considerable physical strength, but was
so well proportioned that one would
not observe it casually, yet his hands
were somewhat small and quite soft,
a peculiarity in his family.

His father was a Virginian—one of the old stock of F. F. V.'s, whose manners and chivalrous customs are fast passing away, along with their eccentricities and follies. Who can tell whether the change is for the better? The man who would not sit in the presence of a lady with his hat on, who would never allow a discourteous word to be spoken of one without resenting it emphatically, and who would champion her cause, is getting to be now a thing of the past. The present utilitarian age is more advanced, but it has lost much of the poetry of life.

His mother was a woman of profound sagacity and sense, with a sweetness of disposition that was unequalled, and withal a gentleness of demeanor that was most attractive. She was very high-spirited, but had herself so thoroughly under control that it was said of her that she was never known to speak ill of any one. The great feature of countenance was her smile. It seemed to light up everything upon which it rested. It had cheered the erring sinner on his death-bed, and had alleviated poverty in its distress. It had calmed an excited multitude and had awed it into peace. Over her household it had exerted an influence that was beyond compare, and her children often looked upon it, in their infancy, as an angel's glance. Could she have been conceived of as an inhabitant of such a sphere, she would have lighted up the horrors of the stygian darkness with the radiance of her smile. It was the unveiling to the outside body of the inside soul.

Randolph Carter had inherited from his father his courtly bearing and demeanor; from his mother he derived that generous disposition and evenness of temperament which so characterized him, together with that perseverance which was one of the true secrets of his success in life. He had been successful. At the close of the great civil war he had found himself a young man, broken in fortune, but with a good name and indomitable perseverance.

He had offered his services to the Confederate Government when he was eighteen, and was immediately made a captain. At the battle of Manassas he had received his first baptism of fire, where he had helped to support Jackson in his hour of need. The seven days' fighting around Richmond had seen him in the thickest of it all, and he led the charge at Malvern Hill when McClellan was driven to his gunboats. At Gettysburg his regiment was amongst those who made an assault which will go down to posterity as one of the famous battles of the world. And finally, when the

sun set upon the war-tossed Con-
federacy at Appomattox, he had
sheathed his sword.

Devoting himself now to peaceful
pursuits, he became identified with the
internal improvement of his country.
The phenomenal development of the
railroad construction throughout the
South afforded him an opportunity of
great usefulness, and his strict integ-
rity and ability finally brought him
into a position of great influence and
considerable means. He was foremost
among the leaders in the movement
that freed the South from the thral-
dom of the carpet-bag legislators,
which the fortunes of war had inflict-
ed upon his people; so, when the new
Administration came into power at
Washington, his opinions were often
consulted and he was one of the
"powers of the throne."

Such was the man she had taken
for an adventurer; such was the be-

ginning of her first acquaintance.
Thus she had repelled him.

As Colonel Carter sat quietly reading his paper, Edyth watched him
particularly. Slowly he appeared to
grow restless, then conscious of something undefinable, until finally he
looked towards her again.

Just then she noticed a lady entering the dining-room and was being shown a seat, when, catching
Colonel Carter's eye, she advanced
towards him. He immediately rose,
shook hands with her in a manner
that Edyth could not but own was
both graceful and courtly, and after
he had spoken to her she took a seat
at the same table. This proceeding
also shocked Edyth's ideas, and she
inwardly estimated the lady as *outre*.

A minute or so later a gentleman
entered, whose appearance interested
her at once. He walked with a decided
military air, and while his general

manner was mild-looking, there was
something about his eye which would
indicate to any close observer that its
possessor was a man of powerful
character. He evidently was a person
of some importance. Persons bowed
to him as he went along, and after he
had passed they turned and looked after him, and pointed him out to each
other. He bowed to her father as he
went by, and, on being ushered where
the lady was sitting, was about to
take a seat beside her, when, catching
sight of Colonel Carter, he gave him
a cordial greeting, then seated himself.

Her father evidently was pleased
at the recognition, and turning to her,
said:

"My daughter, did you notice that
gentleman that bowed to me as he
passed, just now? That man is one
of the noted men of this country.
He is one of the L—s. He was a
famous Confederate general during

the war, and has held high offices of
trust in his State. That lady next
him is his wife."

This piece of information somehow
did not seem to impress her as much
as she thought it might. Here then,
was a famous Confederate brigadier
right before her eyes. He certainly
did not appear as ferocious as he had
been depicted, and from the evident
cordiality of those who had greeted
him, he was regarded with anything
but aversion.

But who was the other gentleman—the one who had spoken to her
and then had left her in so dignified a
manner? After awhile she determined
to ask her father if he knew him. This
she did, but not before making one or
two attempts to do so. Was it accident on her part, or was it some subtle prescience of destiny that her voice
somewhat faltered when she asked
his name?

Her father slowly put on his specs, and gave him an examination so prolonged that Edyth began to feel a little bit uncomfortable that he should scrutinize a stranger so. At last he said: "His face is strangely familiar to me, but I cannot recall his name; I will ask the head-waiter;" for the old gentleman had very readily fallen into the southern custom of asking questions of the head-waiter, who was supposed to know everybody and to be particularly skilful in seating together only persons of congenial acquaintance or disposition.

It was remarkable how shrewd some of the old southern negroes were in this respect. They regarded it as a great feat to be able to tell, by a look, a man they called a gentleman, and it was rare that they were mistaken. It is said of one of these negroes that he was so sagacious that he was given a good salary to remain at the door of a dining-room, his duties being merely to give to the rightful owner his particular hat; and such was his skill in this respect, that, of the many hundreds of hats he delivered during a day, he seldom made a mistake.

Accordingly, Mr. Prescott summoned the head-waiter, and asked the name.

The negro looked first enquiringly; then, on recognizing him, smilingly and with a pomposity that would be amusing were it not for the gravity of his manner, said:

"Dat, sar, am Culn. Randolph Carter. He am, sar, a mity likely gemmun. He am, sar, a first family of Virginny."

That, then, was his name—Randolph Carter! It was a name compounded of family names—names honorably connected with the history of this country.

The love-struck girl, in the ideal

dream of the great English dramatist,
wherein he has drawn a picture which
shall last for all time as the synonym
of a youthful flame, has asked the
question "what's in a name," and
answered herself, by saying that it is
no part belonging to a man, when
she discovered that it was the name
of a hereditary foe. But there is much
in a name. It is sometimes synony-
mous with weakness; again it is coupled with power. Rare are those "immortal names that were not born to
die"—a sinking into oblivion is the
fate of most. Few are coupled with
an honorable mention among all men;
disgrace has characterized the career
of many. But, it is the one grand,
imperishable thing, that a man can
leave to his descendants. Disasters
by war, by fire, or by sea, the treach-
ery of friends, the hostility of enemies,
errors in judgment, and many other
circumstances, may arise to deprive a
man of his fortune. Accidents of va-

rious kinds, sickness, and disease, may
destroy his health; but a good name
is indestructible. It is the monument
more enduring than brass, that a
man can erect to his memory. The
lofty columns of Assyria and the
Rhodean Colossus have crumbled into
dust and disappeared from the face
of the globe; but the Pharaoh who
hardened his heart, and the Sultan
who hardened his head, will hand
down their names to posterity, load-
ed with infamy. The name of the
Lion-Hearted King hushed into silence the awe-struck child of the infi-
del long after the grave had withered
the arm of Cœur de Lion. It is a
glorious thing for one to be able to
say "as long as the language of my
race shall exist, so long will my name
be honored among men; the arch
Destroyer of all animate things can
not destroy my inanimate name. It
is immortal."

Reflections such as these must some-

times come to all men; to Randolph
Carter they were ever recurrent, and
their contemplation had fixed upon
him a concentration of purpose and
elevation of character that raised him
pre-eminent among them.   To those
who knew him as a soldier he was
without fear; without reproach was
his reputation as a man.

When the waiter had finished his
communication he evidently was
pleased. He had kept up his reputation of knowing distinguished men,
and had made an impression upon
his hearers, thus increasing his own
importance. When he had finished,
Mr. Prescott thanked him, and told
his daughter something of the history of the Randolph family, and
also of the Carters.

When breakfast was over, her father proposed a drive around the city,
and later a call upon the President,
to whose levee he had been invited by

the Representative from Massachu-
setts, whom he had met accidentally
in the rotunda of the hotel, and who,
having an eye upon any of his con-
stituents, took advantage of this opportunity of making Mr. Prescott an
ardent partisan ever afterwards.

The drive around Washington was
another revelation to Edyth. She
had seen photographs of the Capitol,
but they had failed to give her any
adequate conception of its proportions, and it was with feelings of
gratified pride that she beheld it. But
already she had met with so much
sight-seeing, and so many new impressions had been stamped upon her
mind, that it was as it were surfeited,
and it was only afterwards that she
realized what she had seen and where
she had been.

At the President's Reception she
found herself in a novel position. At
her home, and when in Europe, owing

to her father's letters of introduction,
she had always moved in the inner
circles of society. At the President's
Reception he had had no particular
card, and therefore they were kept in
what might be called the general
crowd. From the select few in an
interior room she recognized that she
was debarred. In passing by this
door she was taken by surprise on
seeing Colonel Carter there, in quite
an intimate attitude apparently to
those present, and in conversation
with a young lady with whom she
had gone to school, and who she now
recollected was the daughter of a
Cabinet officer. Her school-mate
caught sight of her as she was passing, and immediately went up to
Edyth and brought her into the room,
where she was introduced to those
present.

Colonel Carter had drawn somewhat back when Edyth first entered,

and it was only at the last that, turning to him, her childhood's friend said, "Edyth, I wish to present to you, now, one of the representative men of the South, in whose charge I must leave you, in order to attend to my 'official duties.' You will be in good hands, as he knows everybody in Washington, and can inform you of its celebrities. While under his care you can feel perfectly secure, for he is as noted for his chivalry towards women as he is on record for his bravery among men. Allow me to present to you Colonel Randolph Carter, of Virginia."

CHAPTER III.

WAR OR PEACE.

During the long prelude to this formal introduction, which now satisfied the demands and customs of our present society, Colonel Carter kept his eyes steadily on hers. She thought it never would end; she could not endure his gaze; so her eyes fell towards the floor, and when the name was pronounced, and silence ensued, she merely inclined her body into that position with which a lady acknowledges an introduction, and waited for him to speak. She felt that she had been thrust upon this man, and resented it accordingly, and determined to make him feel it; but she could not think of how in the world to begin. She had never before been at a loss

for something to say, but now she
could not speak a word. When
finally she raised her eyes and met his,
although his facial expression was as
grave as that of a judge, yet she
imagined she detected a merriment in
the expression of his eyes, which she
thought was engendered by the contemplation of her confusion. This
angered her more than ever; still she
could not speak, and she kept on
wondering if he remembered the episode of the breakfast-table. Finally,
when the silence began to be em-
barrassing, he addressed her:

"I can find nothing more original
to say, Miss Prescott, than to ask you
if this is your first visit to Washington?"

This capped the climax with Edyth,
for if there was one idea above all
others she abominated, it was that
she was unacquainted with a place.
She had the one weakness of wishing

to convey the impression that she was
a woman of the world and had somewhat travelled. She was too truthful
to evade a direct question, or to equiv-
ocate, so she was forced to say "yes,"
and this being to her distaste, she
added nothing more.

Another silence ensued, but this
time Colonel Carter spoke sooner than
before, and with the evident desire to
relieve her of her imagined embarrass-
ment, for he told her that she had
then a great treat in store for herself;
that there was much of great interest
in the city, and that, if she would
allow him, he would suggest some
places that it might be profitable for
her to see.

Now Edyth had been very fond of
laying down the law to others, but,
having had her way most of the time
in her father's house, she did not like
the law being laid down for her, and
this seeming assumption of authority

added fuel to the already smouldering
fire. She replied:

"Although this is my first visit to
Washington, yet I am so much of a
traveller that I will be able to investigate it for myself. I could not think
of troubling you to relate to me an
account of things that must be so
familiar to you as to become tiresome
from its familiarity."

As Edyth completed this sentence,
she thought that she had done herself
credit; that she had recovered the
use of her tongue, and that she had
administered what might be called
a mild set-back. She little realized
the character of the man, however,
or the reserve power behind the
quiescent exterior. She noticed that
the look of merriment slowly faded
away, and that it was succeeded
by an expression which can best be
described as that on the face of a
teacher when a favorite scholar is

persistently wilful.   His reply confirmed this, as he said, "So far from
its being a trouble, it would be a
pleasure to me to describe to you the
scenes of which this is a part; but,"
and here he drew his head somewhat
haughtily back, while his nostrils
were slightly compressed, "I would
be loathe to intrude upon you an account of what might be distasteful."

As Edyth had not expected this,
she was not ready for a reply when
he paused.   So he continued

' From your patrician face, I had
imagined you were too used to the
ways of the world, and too much a
philosopher, not to take advantage
of what circumstance and the passing
moment had placed in your power;
but if I have over-estimated your attributes, and formed too high an opinion of your philosophy, I will rectify
my error."

This certainly was more than Edyth

had anticipated. She had been so quick-witted at home that most men there were unwilling to cross swords with her; but here she was at a disadvantage. This reply, so polite yet so caustic in its wording, was uttered in a deliberate manner, which gave an opportunity to modulate a voice naturally susceptible of great intonation. There was certainly a marked compliment, both to her appearance and to her intellect, which gratified her pride; but this was accompanied by a tone so sarcastic as to cut her to the quick. She had evidently met a foeman worthy of her steel; for the first time in her life she had been thrown into confusion, and had been unable to respond with that brilliant repartee for which she was noted. She felt that she must rouse herself and put forth her best exertions. It was war to the knife; she would humiliate this man. While these

thoughts were chasing themselves
through her active mind her eyes
sparkled and flashed, she threw her
head back, which set off to great advantage her fair throat, and poised
it proudly on her shoulders.

Oh! what a picture she would
make as the Venus Victrix, was Colonel Carter's inward thought, as he
stood before her; for he was appreciative of a beautiful woman, espe-
cially so when in such an animated attitude. But he was too good a judge
of human nature, and too true a
reader of character, not to perceive
that she had roused all her energies to
humiliate him. This he determined
to prevent, but he was too chivalrous
to desire to resent it.

The pause that ensued gave Edyth
a chance to recover herself; then she
replied:

"It is the part of true philosophy
to investigate for one's self, and not

take, second hand, the experience of others for one's own. Instead of what you are pleased to call my patrician face, I have your patrician name as the basis for imagining that you should be too much used to the ways of the world as to take advantage of what was my situation."

This staggered the Colonel. He knew by this she recognized him as the offender at the breakfast-table. This, of course, he must ignore. He appreciated the intelligence of the girl, he admired her beauty; but it would never do for her to get the better of him. He had over her the advantage of an extensive acquaintance with the world, a wonderful intuition of character, and experience from several tender episodes with women. She had never loved. She had repelled all the advances of her previous admirers—ridiculing some, refusing others; but she had the

advantage over him that she was a
woman, young and fair, and possessed
of a beautiful face and form.   For
who can estimate the power of a
beautiful woman over mankind?
Did not Achilles' wrath and Ulysses'
shame pay her their tribute on the
Trojan plain?   Did not the Third
Triumvir madly fling away the Western World when, drunk with the
caresses of the Egyptian siren, he fled
from Rome?   Did not the Fifteenth
Louis abandon the affairs of France
and trust the guidance of his mighty
empire to the caprices of his jealous
enchantress?   Have not the saintly
monks run howling to their desert
caves when maddened by the ideal
image of a woman's form?   Have not
the literature and the language of all
men in choicest words portrayed this
theme?   Do not the artist's pencil and
the poet's song attest her power?

As Edyth paused to let the full

effect of her words be felt before continuing, he replied:

"I have promised to rectify my error in regard to your attributes. I already do so as regards your intelligence. I am speaking truthfully when I say that it would be a pleasure to me to describe to you the many phases of Washingtonian life and manners. You must be aware that you are possessed of that which renders you attractive in the eyes of men. Why should I not snatch this moment from the desert of dreary time, as an oasis upon which to enjoy the flying Present? The sped Past is gone beyond recall, while the coming Future is beyond our ken. With you conversing, I would forget all time. I am Epicurean enough to wish to make the most of the present."

"And you wish to make it at my expense," was Edyth's cold reply.

"If you call your edification your

expense," Col. Carter retorted readily, "then I acknowledge that it is
so.. But it is the characteristic of a
good general if he has an advantage
to make the most of it. I vindicate
my claim for generalship by making
use of any advantage that I may
possess."

So far Edyth perceived that she
was not superior to him in command
of language. She had often heard that
Southerners were gifted in this respect, and this experience confirmed it.
She therefore quickly resolved to try
another method of circumventing him,
and, to his discredit be it said, she
instantly accomplished her purpose.
There was no reason why she should
not take advantage of his offer to describe to her the Washingtonians. If
she had been thrust upon him, he
must know it was against her intention or desire. She had given him an
opportunity of getting out of it if he

chose, but he did not seem to wish to get out. Why should she not try the effect of a woman's power upon him? She felt that he was in the humor to be readily influenced by it, and accordingly she determined to use a little strategy, and to draw him on. She was something of an amateur actress, and could simulate a feeling she did not possess. It is a woman's weapon. Therefore, assuming a child-like expression of countenance and glancing at him with an appealing look, she said in a tone modulated to silvery softness:

"It was only on your account, Colonel Carter, that I did not wish to take up so much of your time and attention. It would be not only advantageous, but agreeable, to me to have so accomplished a delineator as yourself. Although it was done ceremoniously, yet I was thrust upon you, and desired to give you a loophole of escape."

The quick indrawing of his breath,
the flash of his eye, and the animation
over his whole countenance, told her
how truly she had hit. Her beauty,
on the apparent abandonment of her
hostile attitude, assumed all that
charm which gentleness gives to a
spirited expression, and he believed
he had subdued her. Oh, how splen-
didly he looks! thought the young
girl, as she noted the effect of her
words; it is wrong in me to lead him
on like this, but he commenced it and
it is nothing more than a man
deserves. If he becomes infatuated
enough to confess a liking for me, and
I then repel him it will be all his own
fault.

To almost any observer, much less
to one of Edyth's close attention, it
was evident that Colonel Carter was
on his mettle. He, too, was closely
observing the countenance of this fair
conspirator. In a tone wonderfully

softened, and with an inflection that now and then struck responsive chords in her feelings, he took up the thread of the narrative. He told her of the many historical incidents connected with the city; how the nations of the Old World were slowly beginning to turn their eyes to this country, as the hinge upon which the world's destiny now hung. He soon caught the key-note of her ambition, and fanned into a glowing flame her slumbering desire to become a factor in the world's progress. With a quickness that was remarkable he indicated some passers-by, and gave her a slight sketch of the character of each. There passed a man she thought was one of the Booths, but he told her that he was the silvery-tongued orator from the Hill City of Virginia. It was he that stopped the rapid degeneration of his party by the mighty eloquence of his words.

He had thundered forth his denuncia-
tions against the party intriguer; he
had kindled an enthusiasm in his fol-
lowers; and when the supreme moment had come he had cast the winning die. A man stood somewhat
near the door, whose attitude she
likened to that of a college professor.
He told her that of this man a distinguished European scientist had
said, that he had made one of the
most transcendent discoveries the
world ever saw. It was he who had
harnessed the human voice, and had
driven it across a continent on a tiny
wire, with the word and the tone
recognizable. A small, elderly, quiet-
looking man next attracted her attention. When Colonel Carter caught
sight of him his voice assumed an
enthusiastic tone that echoed in her
hearing for many a day.

"Were I to tell you the name of that
man, which as the old tale says, be-

gins with a B and ends with an E, I
doubt if you would know of it, as
connected with the great events of
the world's history. That man built
a vessel, and a weapon to defend it,
which undoubtedly would have destroyed all the navies of the previous eras of the world combined
against it. Collect the fleets of Sala-
mis, of Actium, and of Tyre, the Span-
ish Armada, and Trafalgar's ships in
united attack against his single craft,
and they would have gone down like
leaves before an autumn gale. One by
one they would have been destroyed,
powerless to withstand the mighty
blow.

That Edyth was skeptical, and
did not give perfect credence to this
well-attested but little-known historical fact, Colonel Carter soon perceived; therefore he directed her attention to the lighter shades of Washington society. The presence of sev-

eral European adventurers, who were in this country with the avowed purpose of exchanging the empty title of a foreign potentate for the substantial worth of some American heiress, gave him a good opportunity of expressing what most of us have felt. The fact, too, had lately become quite notorious that many reprobates of English society had been taken up at Newport and other fashionable resorts, and had been both feted and entertained by Americans of good standing, who by their toadyism to anything *English* were an object of disgust to sensible people. There is, perhaps, no higher type of the true man than an English gentleman. He is brave, true as steel, and ready to assist in the hour of need. But as everything in Nature has its opposite, so the English gentleman has his antithesis in the adventurer.

This opinion regarding toadyism

to foreigners was particularly pleasing to Edyth, for one of her young
friends had fallen a victim to this
iniquity. Her friend was young, accomplished, handsome, and possessed
of means, when she married a
foreigner—a so-called nobleman. In
two short years she returned to this
country, her fortune squandered, herself broken in spirits and in health,
and in exchange for what proved to
be the merest bauble she gave all of
worth that was hers; and worse than
all, she knew that her one child, beautiful as her heart could desire, carried
in his system the taint of that which
must surely bring him to an untimely
grave, and even during the short time
of life which must be his it would be
embittered by the subtle poison
within him. Edyth always became
indignant when she thought over the
wrongs endured by American women
at the hands of foreigners, and the

manly condemnation of these out-
rages, by Colonel Carter, instead of
the insipid imitation of their customs,
which some of the young men of her
acquaintance had taken up, created a
feeling of liking for him before she was
aware of it.

When the thinning out of the people present indicated to her that it
was time for her to be leaving, too,
it was with dismay that she did not
see her father. Colonel Carter soon
divined this, and he said to her that
it would give him great pleasure to be
allowed to accompany her to the
hotel.

Now, Mr. Prescott, of late years,
had become somewhat absent-minded.
He had met at the levee some old
friends, and became so interested in
his new surroundings that he had
left the White House, forgetting that
his daughter had accompanied him
there.

When Edyth found this out, and
when she had been assured that Mrs.
Grundy would be satisfied with her
returning with Colonel Carter on account of his well-known position, she
consented to his accompanying her.
As they passed through the streets on
that bright afternoon, it was strange
to her that of so many people she
should not know any, yet her companion should have so large a circle
of acquaintance. Men in uniform,
and in citizen's dress, handsome
women, and foreigners, saluted him
as he passed by, and the recognition
was always accompanied by a friendly
greeting.   A woman always feels
proud if the man she is with is one of
distinction; and while this was the
case with her present companion, yet,
even when returning the recognition
of his acquaintance, he never relaxed
his attention to her. This gratified
her pride.   She was beginning to

make this man her devoted admirer. Soon she would have him an urgent suitor.

As they approached the hotel he said to her, "I have snatched from Father Time a brief interval, whose contemplation will relieve the dreariness of many a future hour. Recalling the memory of this meeting, I can evoke from the depths of my inner consciousness a pleasure, of which no future fate can deprive me. I must now bid you farewell. It is probable that in the course of future events I will never see you again, as our paths lie divergent ways. I will close this event of my life by an adaptation from my favorite author:

"My only love sprung from my only hate,
"Too early seen, unknown, and known too late."

CHAPTER IV.

ON TO RICHMOND.

When Colonel Carter uttered these last words he raised his hat and bowed, and left her before she had time to speak to him again. She stood looking at his retreating form; then recollecting herself, immediately entered the hotel. This, then, was the end of it all. They were never to meet again; where was her triumph now; what good had it done her to have made this man momentarily show a weakness? Somehow it saddened her to think that she would never see him again, and she half-way regretted that the interview had not been prolonged. If her woman's power had him under its spell for the time being, was not his good-by an

equivalent, in that it made her continue to think of him? Such a revery
she felt would never do, and she therefore shook it off, with that firm
resolve of purpose which is so characteristic of the descendants of the
Puritans.

The next morning, when Mr. Prescott suggested their resuming their
trip, it was with a reluctant feeling
that she consented. They engaged
their seats in the car early, and having a little time to wait, they visited
the spot consecrated as the place
where the maniac assassin had struck
down the Chief Magistrate of the
nation. They observed with curiosity
the many different ways that passers-
by regarded the star. Some protected
themselves with the sign of the Holy
Cross, others elevated their eyes to
heaven as if in prayer; none stepped
over it.

On the train Edyth noticed, directly

opposite her, an exceedingly pretty
young girl, who was surrounded by
a bevy of young men, bidding her
good-by. She probably had been
on a visit to Washington from some
neighboring locality, and was now
returning. Presently Edyth overheard
one of them say to her that she had
some one's seat, to which she rather
demurely replied, that if she did she
reckoned whoever it was would not
eat her up; at which one of the more
forward of her admirers said that she
was so sweet he did not see how the
owner of the seat could help eating
her up, at which sally of wit all
laughed. This did not harmonize
with Edyth's feelings at the moment
at all, and, if the truth were told, it
is probable that she looked down upon
this innocent conversation with dis-
dain. Her father had secured a seat
in front of hers.

Presently she saw two gentlemen

enter. Even a moment's glance sufficed to show her that one was the man whose image had haunted her so persistently. Why was it that the color rushed so unbidden to her face, and that she felt an over-burdened and oppressed feeling? As the elder of the two gentlemen drew near to the young lady who had attracted her attention, she overheard him say:

"Caroline; I wish to introduce to you an old friend of mine, Colonel Randolph Carter, and I desire to place you under his charge until you arrive at Fredericksburg, where the carriage will meet you. Colonel, this is the young lady who was so fond of you when she was a little child, and who was wont to call you her sweetheart."

At this somewhat novel form of introduction Edyth expected to see the young lady in question covered with confusion. So far from this, it appeared as if she was quite used to such, and merely held out her hand, which Colonel Carter, it seemed to Edyth, took with pleasure, and lingered over much longer than there was any necessity for.

Colonel Carter told her, in a few words, how glad he was to see her again, and complimented her on how much she had grown, both in size and appearance. He further said, laughingly, that she must behave, or else he would scold her, at which her father smiled.

The two gentlemen moved on, and Edyth overheard her say, with a toss of her pretty head, "put me under his charge, indeed; he had better be put under my charge. I tell you what, I'll wager anything I'll make him make love to me before I get to Fredericksburg." At which the chorus of her admirers acquiesced, and the forward one vowed that he only wished he was in Colonel Carter's place—that he would make love to her without any compulsion.

When the two gentlemen passed her father, the elder recognized him, and stopped to exchange a few words, during which interval she saw Colonel Carter introduced to her father, and take his seat beside him; while the father of the young girl, after bidding her good-by, left the train, seemingly perfectly satisfied after having put his daughter under Colonel Carter's care.

As the train drew out from the depot, Edyth observed Colonel Carter glance at his fair charge, but as she had a companion beside her, he kept his seat. Soon she observed that he and her father became engaged in earnest conversation. Evidently Colonel Carter was describing the various points of interest. Now and then parts of the conversation came to her sufficiently audibly to make them out.

4

She overheard the words Long Bridge
and Wilkes Booth, and then she imagined that this must have been the route
by which the actor escaped across the
river, after shooting the President.
She would have liked to have heard
what Colonel Carter was saying, in
order to infer what was his opinion
about that deed, which she had always
regarded as a most heinous crime.
He evidently was deeply impressed
with the gravity of the subject, and
was speaking most regretfully about
it and condemning it.

When the cars stopped at Alexan-
dria the conversation became more
distinct. She overheard the anecdotes
about the seizure of the town, about
the exploits in that neighborhood of
the noted scout whose experiences
and hair-breadth escapes were so remarkable as to hardly bear credence,
yet whose after-career in the Holy
Church stamped all his utterances as

those of the truth. Then there was
Bull Run creek, until evidently her
father was completely given up to
listening to his companion's words.

Over and over again Edyth tried to
fix her attention upon a book, but that
she could not do. Her mind would
go to wondering what they were saying; then she tried to make out
whether Colonel Carter knew of her
presence or not. Did he associate her
father's name with her own, and did
he, knowing this, studiously avoid
her? He had had his back always to
her, and it was uncertain whether he
had seen her or not. Then the boast
of that pretty little child (for Edyth
could not but regard her as anything
else) kept ringing in her ears. Could
a person of so staid and dignified
an appearance as Colonel Carter, and
of such evident strength of character,
be so frivolous as to outrage the
sacred feeling, love, by discoursing

of it in a chance meeting like this! Edyth was unaware how lightly Southern girls will talk about this subject, and how, seemingly, they will jest about it. She was ignorant of how much true feeling has been covered up by this flippant exterior, or how nobly the Southern women would respond to the call of duty. She failed to realize what the author of Waverly has immortalized in such choice language, when he undertook to describe "woman in her hours of ease."

After following the windings of the Potomac for about an hour, during which time many opportunities were afforded her of taking in its never-to-be-forgotten scenery, Edyth observed the cars leave the river and take a direction into the interior.

When Colonel Carter discovered this he spoke a few words to her father, of a somewhat different nature

from what he had been previously
saying; then he got up and approached the young lady who had
been put under his charge. As he
drew near to her she put on a most
aggrieved look, and asked him if he
was not ashamed to have deserted
her so; that she was afraid of being
left to her own devices—all this being
accompanied by a bewitching look of
helplessness.

"Oh! what a little story-teller,"
was Edyth's inward comment, as the
whole of this conversation became
audible to her, and she wondered if
Colonel Carter would be taken in by
such artfulness. Whatever the Colonel thought, he was too much of an
adept to be off his guard, or not ready
with his answer.

"Whatever fear, Miss Carrie, you
may have had at your own devices,
I had still greater fear of them, and
kept out of harm's way; for if I had

suffered myself to be exposed to your fascination I would have fared but badly at your hands."

This flattery was evidently pleasing, as she again essayed to "try the art of powerful beauty on that warrior's heart," and it was very evident to Edyth that she was merely endeavoring to make good her boast.

"Will he be goose enough to be cajoled into it?" was Edyth's half-contemptuous query, as she quietly watched the moves and counter-moves of this little by-play.

No woman likes to see another receive all the attention from the gentleman present; and while in her case there was abundant good reason for it, still it was none the less unpleasant to Edyth to see this little chatterbox monopolize every one.

Soon, however, Fredericksburg was reached; and Colonel Carter, after having disposed of his charge,

came back into the car and said something to her father. He appeared to
acquiesce with some sort of a proviso,
and both approached her. She pre-
tended to be reading her book, and
only looked up when her father spoke.

"Edyth," he said, "this is the
town of Fredericksburg. In this very
place one of the greatest battles of
the late war was fought. The train
will be detained here about two
hours, and while we are waiting I
propose we walk over the battle-field.
This gentleman, Colonel Carter, of
Virginia, has kindly promised to accompany us and point out some of
the salient features."

Here was another long prelude to
an introduction to this man. She felt
his gaze upon her face, though she
persistently looked at her father while
he was speaking; when he ceased she
looked towards Colonel Carter, and
again merely bowed, leaving it to him
to commence the conversation.

A slight pause ensued, during which Edyth's thoughts again chased one another like wildfire. Did he recognize her? Did he remember the breakfast-table at the hotel, or how he had bade her good-by? All these and many others flashed through her mind quicker than the speech which could utter them.

Colonel Carter spoke in an accentuated tone of voice, but without the slightest sign of recognition in his manner, as he said that it would give him pleasure to go over the ground with her; that the place was so familiar to him as to become almost burdensome from its familiarity, and therefore he thought he could point out the position of the two armies to her with great accuracy.

He did recognize her, then! By quoting the words of their previous meeting he showed to her that recognition in a way that she alone could understand. Why had he not spoken

to her before in the cars, and why did
he acknowledge the acquaintance in
such a round-about manner? It appeared to Edyth as if he was trying
to tantalize her, and she accordingly
resolved to pay him back in his own
coin. But how was she to get the opportunity? As they walked out from
the streets of Fredericksburg, and, after passing a valley, began climbing
the hill up whose sides one of the finest
armies of modern times precipitated
itself headlong against an entrenched
foe, Edyth could not but admire the
skill and eloquence of her companion
in describing the terrible scene. Here
was the very wall up to whose edge
some few had reached, even although
the great mass of their support had
been driven back by the leaden hail.
Off in the distance was the stand
where the two guns of the young ar-
tillerist had been placed, from whose
iron throats death-dealing canister

had been belched, which mowed down
the ranks of the invaders like hay before a scythe. On the crest of the hill
had been the man who, "standing
like a stone wall," had added to his
name a title more lofty than any con-
ferred by puissant royalty. On the
hills across the river had been planted
the opposing artillery. Colonel Carter's face fairly glowed with sup-
pressed excitement as he told of the
final charge and its repulse, and then
the headlong rush of the victors as
they drove the enemy back out of
their lines.

As Edyth listened to his descrip-
tions it seemed to her as if she could
evoke from the quiet hills the spirits
of the silent dead; that in her mind's
eye she could see the mighty hosts as
they locked in their deadly embrace;
and could hear the roar of the distant
guns. It did not take his final *quo-
rum pars fui* for her to realize that

Colonel Carter had been there, too.
How different he looked now than
when she first saw him.   She saw him
now—the soldier and the hero that he
was—and oh! how her heart warmed
towards him on his conclusion as he
said:

"When the sun set at Appomattox
Courthouse the warlike episodes of
my life sunk into their eternal grave.
The great principles for which I fought
were determined by the arbitrament
of the sword. The decision of the
sword was against me, and I accepted
its results as conclusive. I took up
the pen to aid in redeeming my country, as far as my limited abilities
would allow, from the awful desolation that was upon it. When you
recollect that all the money represented by the Confederate bonds and
notes; all the railroad, bank and
insurance company's stocks; all the
property represented by farming im-

plements, horses, and cattle, were
swept from existence, you can form
only a small idea of what the condition of things actually was. The
unholy order had been faithfully observed, that through these beautiful
valleys such destruction should be
done that even the crow must carry
its provisions in its flight in order to
avoid starvation When you think
on this, add to such a desolation the
ten-fold worse incubus of the large
class of harpies who settled themselves upon this country, and were
immediately seated in legal power on
account of the disfranchisement of
the only intellectual class. I myself
have heard one of them say, on the
eve of a great political election, when
addressing a crowd of the recently-
enfranchised freedmen, *if you do not
win at the ballot-box, matches are
only five cents; you can burn down
their barns and dwellings, and smoke*

them out. When seated in legislative halls these worse than vultures plunged their States into irretrievable ruin. They ordered such things as spittoons, giving one hundred dollars apiece for them, and pocketed the spoils. Debts heaped upon a State by such unhallowed practices like these were themselves sufficient to destroy a community, but when you add to such the further condition of the existing desolation of the land, you will realize that the outlook was indeed wrapped in gloom. Day after day I have listened to the voice of woe, until my spirit was almost sunk in despair." "But," and here Colonel Carter drew himself up to his full height, and his voice came as ringing and clear as if the consciousness of an entire rejuvenation was now upon him—he continued, "I never lost faith in my country's future. I could not but believe that my surviving comrades saw the dawn of light as I did, and when the darkest hour had passed we put our united shoulders to the wheel with a solid effort. The South of to-day is totally different from the South of a quarter of a century ago. The same sun is there, but it sets upon a different epoch. The evening and the morning were the next day. Some have called this epoch the New South. Whatever it is, it is the return of prosperity to this fair land once more. When a few more days of warm spring sunshine comes upon us you will see the land put forth its increase, and two blades of grass will grow where one only was growing before."

He ceased speaking and a dead silence ensued. Mr. Prescott was thinking whether it was really so that Northern men had instigated the negroes to barn-burning and such swindling. Edyth was thinking of how totally different this man's character was from her first idea. Colonel Carter was thinking of the unalterable past. A warning whistle notified them that it was time to return to the train.

As they went along Colonel Carter said to her in a voice whose tones somehow seemed to linger in her hearing like as the echo from distant hills when softened by the lapse of time:

"Miss Prescott, I am aware that introductions in Washington society are sometimes considered as nothing, and that persons are at liberty to disregard them afterwards if they desire it. Will you not allow me to make an exception to this, and base a claim of old acquaintance on account of my being introduced to you there?"

"So you do condescend to recognize me at last?" was Edyth's cold reply to this friendly overture.

She had begun to have quite a liking

for Colonel Carter, founded on what
he had narrated, and was angry with
herself for having this liking. Again,
she was piqued at his not having
spoken to her before, or taken any
previous cognizance of their introduction. After she had said the words
she became aware of how harsh they
were, and would have changed them,
but it was too late, and, moreover,
sarcasm was her very strong point,
and she wished to draw him into
giving her an opportunity of using it.

"I might have given you the option
of recognizing me," was Colonel Carter's rejoinder, "but I never could have
so outraged my inner feelings or per-
ceptions as to forget you. Condescension must come from you. It is not
becoming in me."

The gauntlet was again thrown
down. How exasperating it was to
think that in this cool and gentlemanly
way he could put her down. She be-

came horror-struck at the thought
that she might have fallen unconsciously into liking him, while he apparently was absolutely indifferent to
her. Had she known the truth she
might have done differently, or had
she known of Colonel Carter's subtle
power she might have concealed her
feeling more. He was one of those
very few persons who possess the mys-
terious faculty of reading intuitively
another's thought. Call it by any
name one might choose, there was
something communicating between
other persons' minds and his which
enabled him to interpret the thought.
He could not tell himself how he possessed this power, or wherein it lay.
All he knew was, that at times an
overpowering sense came upon him,
and with it a divination of the
thoughts of others. This was not always manifest, or existent, but under
certain conditions it became devel-

oped. As regards Edyth it began to
be manifest in a pre-eminent degree.
It may have been what the Greek
tried to portray in his "Force of the
Soul." There was no chance for sarcasm now; he had completely turned
the tables upon her; and, worse than
this, she began to fear that she was
no match for him in a linguistic en-
counter. Instead, therefore, of retalia-
tion, she put the entire onus upon him
by saying:

"Since you clothe me with powers
of condescension, I will use them by
granting you immunity for having so
cavalierly ignored me."

If Colonel Carter had had the advantage over her before, he lost it
now. He felt called upon to make up
for his neglect of this fair young girl,
and it was very far from being a
disagreeable task. He took the seat
beside her in the car, and did not
leave it during the remainder of the

trip to Richmond. If he was a man of the world, and had seen its most varied features, she was young and beautiful, conscious of her beauty, and skilful in the use of its power. The idle boast of her fellow-traveller kept ringing in her ears and continually suggesting, Why not make this courtly man address her; why not make him a victim of her beauty? why not lead him on? She would curb his haughty spirit, even if in so doing she broke his heart.

Whether Colonel Carter divined these thoughts or not, he again put forth all his efforts to please. She had nothing to complain of now—no ignoring of her presence. He touched on the various scenes of interest as they passed along—of where the Great Soldier had died, and how the whole line was hallowed with memories of past events. Each subject, as he touched upon it, seemed

clothed with a new light. Yet this
was not done in an ostentatious way.
It was the quiet unfolding of his
views and thoughts to her. He spoke
without reserve, and almost unconsciously, for it seemed as if language
flowed from his tongue as liquid as
honey. So well did he fulfil this task
that it hardly appeared but a few
minutes before the train was passing
through a town whose stately trees
and shaded walks reminded her somewhat of Cambridge. She was surprised, too, to see students coming
out from buildings which appeared as
dormitories. She interrupted Colonel Carter in his narratives, to enquire
about this village, for she was unaware that a college of much excel-
lence was being developed in a place
of which she had never heard. He
informed her that it was the town of
Ashland.

Again, a few minutes had scarcely

elapsed, when the face of the country gradually changed and became more open, and presently tall, slender church-steeples pierced the blue azure of the outline of the sky, while underneath the roofs of buildings and smoke from chimneys indicated their approach to a city. Edyth had no conception of the topography of the country. In all her ideas of Richmond she had imagined it a low-lying city, surrounded by flat lands and waste woods. Her surprise was great when she found it what it is. This was the city of which she had heard so much and knew so little. This long, broad street, down which the train was passing, was apparently unending, and what a beautiful park, what fine residences, and how bright the sun was reflected from the large windows. Presently the train shot into a tunnel, from which it emerged and soon came upon the long bridge

across the James. What a sight, to
see the water breaking over the rocks
and glittering like streaks of light,
and how high the train was up in the
air; what colossal foundries were
underneath, and what a romantic and
picturesque castle on top of the hill
overlooking the river!

It was almost painful when Colonel Carter broke in upon her reverie
by telling her that the ideal must
make way for the real, and that,
as they were at the station, he would
now bid her good-by. She was partly
dazed by the approach to Richmond
being so different from anything that
she had previously conceived. She
did not take in the situation, and he
had raised his hat and gone before
she realized that he was about to go.

As he turned away she felt a curious
sensation; an oppression about the
heart seemed to extend to her entire
body, and things began to grow dim

before her.   By a mighty effort of her
indomitable pride she threw it off.
Never would she acknowledge to herself or let others surmise that the going of any man was a matter of
moment to her. She answered her
father with an alertness that was
almost overdone, and drove to the
hotel without betraying a sign. Yet
she felt stung. He might at least
have asked where they were going,
or expressed a desire to meet again.
He was at home, she a stranger in the
city of his nativity, and he might
have shown them some little courtesy.
He might have indicated to her father
where were some objects of interest.

The dinner at the Exchange was a
mockery to her. She could not do
more than taste the food, but it was
pleasant to see how the guests of the
hotel were looked after by the proprietor; and later in the afternoon she
felt quite at home with his wife, who

took such a kind interest in her comfort. As her father soon met some
gentleman who courteously entered
into conversation with him, she was
left to her own resources; so she
started out for a short walk, but the
lengthening shadows of the dying day
warned her to return almost immediately. Her impressions of the city
were very much mixed She had heard
of the electric railway, which had accomplished such a revolution in as-
cending hills and going around sharp
curves; so she thought she would ride
on it a little way. The car was full
as she entered, but she had hardly
gotten inside the door when a man
jumped up, and, touching his hat,
said, "Won't you take this seat?"
Edyth was annoyed at this, as she
did not know what to do, and the man,
though very kind in his manner, was
in his appearance a laborer. So she
declined the seat and remained stand-

ing. She noticed that she soon became an object of attention, and to
avoid this quietly left the car and got
into the next one, which was not full.
As it went along, however, it soon
filled, and then she observed how in-
variable the custom was. No matter
what the condition of the person,
when a lady entered she was immediately given a seat. Edyth was particularly pleased at having found out
this by her own observation; so, having ridden until she came to the great
broad street that she imagined must
be the same one on which she had
come down in the train, she retraced
her steps to the hotel. Her surprise
again was great as, on entering the
Capitol Square, and before being
aware of it she was face to face with
the famous statue of Washington,
which ornaments its grounds. Seated
on his impatient horse, she saw out-
lined against the evening sky the

5

embodiment in bronze of him who was first in war, first in peace, and first in the hearts of his countrymen. His face was calm and dignified but full of power. The mighty sword which had broken the invader's power hung sheathed at his side, while the hand that had wielded the mightier pen was lifted, pointing to the west. High on his seat of martial state, which far outshone the pose of eloquence and law, or where the forest state with generous hand hid in her shades the hunter's spoils and game, the chief, exalted, sat by merit raised to that proud eminence. Below him was the orator whose words had fired the land, and the judge whose pen had fixed the law. The tongue of the mighty orator who defied the maniac king was stilled forever, but his appeal for liberty stood embodied in immortal form. His outstretched arms remain encased in the metal's fold.

awaiting the receipt of the priceless boon.

It was some time before Edyth could bring herself to leave this group, and it was with feelings far different from those of the beginning that she ended her walk. Her spirits were elated. The enthusiasm of youth had overcome the disappointment of the day. When she went to her room she saw that a bright fire had been lighted, and that the room was cheerful and warm. She sat down in the twilight and mused over the day's adventures. Why was it that the thought of one man kept haunting her mind, or that she could not banish his image from her recollection? Even in this room there seemed to be something that spoke of him—that told her that he was here. A feeling of restlessness hitherto unknown took possession of her. She must get rid of it, and with this in view she rose to dress, in order to go down to the parlor. As she lighted the gas and approached the bureau she saw a letter lying on it, as if waiting. At first she was momentarily startled, but, seeing her name, took it up mechanically. There was no mistaking that the letter was for her. In a firm, bold hand her name was written, and the envelope was in due form. She turned it over in her hand and saw, where it was sealed, one of those crests which are generally used by families in the South—the motto, written in Latin, she readily translated, "forever true." Before opening it, she wondered who could be the writer. Suddenly it flashed across her mind that it might be from Colonel Carter, for who else could have written her Eagerly she tore open the envelope, and a moment's disappointment took possession of her as she saw no signature; but a glance at the contents corrected this. It read as follows;

"Mr. Randoiph Carter presents his compliments to Miss Prescott, and requests that she will allow him the pleasure of taking her to drive tomorrow at twelve. Miss Prescott need not trouble herself to send an answer, as Mr. Carter will call in person this evening at eight."

A thrill of triumph passed through her as she read this note. He had not intended to let her visit his city without showing her some little attention. He had evidently found out somehow where she was stopping, and had done so without asking her. Was this an accident on his part or was it design? His manner towards her had been tender. Was it true? His family motto seemed to answer that question. Tender and true. The words of the old song kept ringing in her ears. "Tender and true." Tender and true. It seemed as if the entire room was full of reminiscences of him. To escape from this she went down stairs, wondering what her father would say to her going to drive, and, to her relief, met the wife of the proprietor on the way down.

Edyth accordingly asked her whether this was customary. The old lady enquired who it was that had asked her, and on Edyth's telling, said:

"Law, child, of course you can go with him, and you will have a good time, too. I would as lief a daughter of mine should go to the north pole with him, if she could get back the same day. Why, I brought Ranny Carter up, and I knew his father and his grandfather, too."

With this the kind-hearted old lady entered into a long description of the Carters; for it always delighted her to have a good listener, and Edyth proved an excellent one on this occasion.

On asking her father's permission, the old gentleman replied that the manners and customs at the South were somewhat different from those at the North; that here persons had often known one another from childhood, and that even their grandparents had been cronies; so there was more freedom of association. He finally ended by leaving the matter to Edyth, saying, however, that her aunt would join them in a day or so, and that such matters must be left to her superior judgment afterwards.

There is a sort of superior consciousness when a young girl knows that some one is coming to see her in the evening—that she and she alone is the attraction, and, that she knows of the coming and no one else. This feeling, so beautifully idealized in the old song, was intensified in Edyth by her present surroundings. She was in a strange place, and impressions were crowding upon her, and foremost among these was the impress of an image that was constantly being brought before her. She looked forward to the meeting, and did what many a girl has done before—watched the minute hand of the dial as the time went by. How well she recollected the allusion to the flight of time when they were together at Washington, and now it was upon her. She went to her room, so as not to be on the spot in advance, and when the knock came upon the door she took a minute or two before answering. As the card was presented by the waiter, she carelessly tossed it on the table and told the servant to to say that she would be down soon. Her spirits were high when she descended the stairway, and the color in her cheeks rose rapidly as she approached the parlor door. There was

a keen sense of something—was it
disappointment—when, as she entered, she saw her father talking to
Colonel Carter. As she advanced to-
ward him and caught his eye the
lighting up of his face was magical.
There was a look of keenest pleasure,
and over it came that smile that she
recalled so well. How her heart did
beat; she felt as if its beat could almost be heard; and as he came to
meet her there was something so gentle in his manner that it touched her
to the core. She again dropped her
eyes, for it seemed to her that she
could not meet his gaze.

With a tone so different from that
which he had used on the train, and
whose softness so well harmonized
with his manner, he enquired how she
was. Soon after receiving her assent
to the drive he rose to bid her good-
night, and as he did so he told her
that he wished to take her father to

the club, so as to introduce him to
some of his friends, and whose acquaintance might make his visit to
the city more pleasant.

She had wronged him, then, in her
former opinion; he had not intended
that her visit to his city should go by
unheeded, and he had arranged to
make it pleasant for her father. This
conviction that she had wronged him
impelled her generous spirit to make
amends, and therefore she allowed in
her manner a more friendly attitude
than any she had yet assumed.

Colonel Carter was quick to see
this. While unconscious of the motive,
he saw the result. Speaking low, so
that none but she could hear, he said:
"Good-night; a hotel parlor is no fitting place in which to tell that which
my tongue finds ready for its utterance; an audience such as this must
not hear that which is for your ear
alone. I must say good-night; the

force of present circumstance is such
that I am constrained to leave your
presence, but when to-morrow's sun
shall have climbed his greatest height
I will return; till then adieu."

CHAPTER V.

THE DRIVE.

The next day broke clear and cloud-
less. It was one of those days in early
spring that so gladden the heart. The
bright sun and warm wind made all
nature respond to their vivifying effect,
and man himself, with all his artificial
surroundings, could not but feel elated
at nature's outburst. Mr. Prescott
was down early. He had passed a
most agreeable evening, and as he met
his daughter somewhat amused her
by giving an account of his experiences. Most particularly was he
impressed with the secretary of a historical society, who, happening to be
quite phenomenal in his line, put him
entirely in the background by his
knowledge of the early history of the

country and of the genealogies and reminiscences of the families of the early settlers. He had been particularly pleased when, making a Latin quotation apropos of the subject under discussion, which he was afraid might not be understood, he found his listener not only appreciative, but capable of adding to it by the continuance of the quotation. He found out that he had been greatly deceived in his opinion of the Southern people, and he started back to the club soon after breakfast, to continue this acquaintance, leaving his daughter to her own devices.

She took a walk along the streets and tried to imagine how they looked when filled with the many soldiers that had passed through them. She pictured to herself Colonel Carter at the head of his column, and wondered whether he would have checked the rush of his troops, in order to save her from harm, had he suddenly come upon her on the field of battle.

She came upon two pillars of stone before an armorial-looking building, supporting two large stone balls; and she wondered if projectiles of this size could be fired from a cannon, and how they would hew down everything before them. About eleven she returned to the hotel and prepared for the drive. As the time approached, a strange nervousness kept creeping over her, but she steadily resisted it. Just before twelve she went down on the bridge connecting the two hotels and seated herself by the window. This bridge, so unique in its structure, has witnessed many a curious scene. Spanning the street between the two hotels, and uniting them into one, it affords a good view of the two approaches. Over its floors have passed many of the distinguished men of the State. It is a favorite place for travel-

lers, in wnich to sit and view the passers-by, and for the gossips to retail
their choicest stories. Near by were
seated two girls, who were evidently
familiar with their surroundings, and
who were discussing the last party
which they attended. The feeling of
nervousness increased upon Edyth as
the time drew near; and summon her
resolution as she might, she could not
prevent a tremulous motion of her
hands. Finally, as a neighboring
clock struck twelve she saw a pair of
horses enter the street at the Capitol
Square and draw near. Long before
she could make out the features of the
occupant of the drag, she overheard
one of the girls say to the other:

"Look, Ida, there comes Randolph
Carter. I do believe he is coming to
take me out driving."

To which her companion somewhat
unfeelingly replied, "I don't believe
any such thing; I don't reckon he has

leisure enough to be taking us girls
driving, for they say he is kept very
busy. See, he is going to stop at the
hotel, however.''

By this time Edyth fully recognized
him, but his horses continued to rear
so as to keep his attention fixed on
them and leave him no opportunity
of looking away.

"He has got his tiger with him,"
one of the girls remarked, "and if I
was going with him I would'nt want
that little jackanapes seated behind
me listening to everything that was
being said. I couldn't talk at all."

"I wouldn't mind that," the other
added; "you may depend on it that
little darkey is as keen as a briar, and
has too much sense to hear things. I
have heard that he is deaf and dumb,
but I don't believe it. I have seen
Colonel Carter speak to him; however, he may have understood from
the motion of the lips; but, boy or no

boy, if he has come for me, I am going."

During this dialogue Edyth was
secretly pleased at the certainty that
Colonel Carter had come for her.
She saw one of the servants hurry
down to the drag and take a card,
while something was being repeated
to him, so as to fix it in his mind;
then, as the servant turned away, she
noticed Colonel Carter give a sign to
the boy. Up to this time he had sat
still as a statue. With his arms folded
and his eyes straight in front of him,
he had balanced himself to the sway-
ing motion of the drag most skilfully.
At the sign, the little fellow became
all motion. He appeared almost to
fly down from his seat, and, seizing
the check-rein of the horses, he held
on to them notwithstanding their
plunging, sometimes being lifted off
his feet. Edyth's blood ran cold, for
she momentarily expected to see him

trampled under foot; but he did not show the slightest sign of fear, nor did Colonel Carter appear at all uneasy at his position. The servant now handed her the card with another famous flourish, and as he did so he said, "de our an de man am cum"; with this he fairly grinned from ear to ear. Edyth's nervousness was now at its height, but she bravely forced it down. Hastily descending, so as to give herself no time to think, she met Colonel Carter at the door, with a composure which astonished herself, but which he was observant enough to detect was forced. At sight of her the horses plunged again, until it seemed as if they would tear themselves to pieces. Colonel Carter handed her in, then seated himself beside her, taking the reins instantly. As he folded the buggy robes around her, the prancing of the horses really alarmed her. Unconsciously she took hold of Colonel Carter's arm, as if for protection.

A reassuring smile passed over his face as he asked, "Are you afraid?"

Even in this supreme moment of excitement Edyth did not forget the woman. Looking straight into his face, with that look of confidence he had learned to know so well, and which had stirred him to the depths of his very soul, she replied:

"Not when with you; I am only a a little unused to the situation."

Beyond a slight indrawing of the breath there was no outward sign that the words had had any effect, but she saw that the arm which held the reins was slightly shaking. In defence of Colonel Carter, be it said, that she was looking gloriously beautiful. The excitement had sent the blood mantling to her cheeks, and had given a brilliancy to her eye which was magnificent. When a woman

like that allows a man to perceive
that she is leaning upon him, it is
enough to unsteady his nerves. He
merely said:

"That is enough; you need not
fear."

The words were simple, but the
voice in which they were spoken con-
veyed the reassurance. Edyth had
observed that during this time the
horses kept tugging away at the bits;
but the boy, instead of watching
them, was watching Colonel Carter.
He gave him another sign, and at the
same time spoke to the horses. The
noble animals instantly plunged forward and they were off before she
knew it. Her attention was so taken
up with the start, and it was so sudden, that she supposed the groom had
been left behind. She was astonished
on looking around to see him seated
behind, stiff as a statue, with his
arms folded but with his eyes spark-

ling like diamonds. She could best liken his expression to that of a highly-trained pointer, waiting for the word of command before starting the game. After the first square or two she became more accustomed to the movement and felt less alarm. Colonel Carter was a splendid driver, and his horses obeyed his word of command notwithstanding their many cavortings. Edyth noticed that they were traversing an uninviting part of the city, but supposed it was on the route to the more fashionable quarter, when, to her surprise, Colonel Carter reined his horses up before a low, ugly-looking building on what she thought was the river's edge, and asked her to examine it critically.

Of course she inferred that it must be a famous building, and that he wished her to see it first before telling her what it was. He got out of the

buggy and took her into the various
rooms, which were redolent of powerful chemical fertilizers; and then they
walked around the outside, where she
could take in the exterior. Across the
street was the canal, and beyond that
the river's edge, where everything was
joyous with the reanimating life of a
budding spring-time.

Finally Edyth could no longer re-
strain her curiosity, and said, "I must
confess, Col. Carter, that your taste
in selecting this building, either as an
interesting one or as one illustrative
of this country, appears remarkable
to me, unless, it may be, that your
countrymen are so devoted to agricul-
ture that they delight in such incon-
gruities."

"Do you see anything so horrible
about the building or the location?"
Colonel Carter enquired, as she paused
for him to reply.

"No, I do not," was the frank response. "I would not select it as a site for a fashionable dwelling, with all these factories around it; but it has the open sunlight and the open air on all four sides, and I do not see anything so terrible about it," for she had now guessed that something awful must be connected with the history of the building, and that Colonel Carter was about to give an account of foul murder and outrage.

"That is Libby Prison," he quietly explained.

Edyth did not at first think he was in earnest. This building was so different from the dark and loathsome structure that her imagination had conjured up as the picture of this prison that it was some time before she could realize that this indeed was the veritable structure. Of course this city was Richmond, and this must be the place. Colonel Carter gave her time to take it in again; then said:

"There has been such a vast amount
of misconception, misrepresentation,
and falsehood connected with that
building, that it is almost impossible
to eliminate from one's mind precon-
ceived ideas, and to take in the facts
as they were. In the outset, I will
admit that at times the provisions
furnished the prisoners were very
scarce, and of unaccustomed quality,
and that the prison was often over-
crowded; but these things were not
the fault of the Southern authorities.
At times food could not be obtained.
I have it on the authority of the officer
who was in charge of that depart-
ment, that the food furnished the
prisoners in Libby was identical with
that issued to the Southern troops in
the field. I myself, at one time, was
three days without any rations whatever, and subsisted on corn, which I
took from the field and parched with
fire made of pine tags, my only drink

being water from the way-side ditches.
You can hardly believe to what terrible straits we were sometimes driven.
As to the overcrowding of the prisons,
the authorities at the North would
not agree to an exchange of prisoners,
hoping by this means to break down
the power of the South by not allowing such reinforcements to be returned."

"But these are the horrors of war,"
he resumed, when, on ceasing to speak,
she made no motion of interruption.
"There were many ludicrous phases
of life, which came in as a bright spot
upon the utter darkness of those trying times. Many false stories about
this prison have been started in fun,
and in order to puff up one's own importance. I met a curious illustration
of that a month or so after the cessa-
tion of hostilities, when, in a little village in New England, I was conversing
with a lady who was very bitter

against the South, and particularly
so on account of this prison. I asked
her where she got her information
from, as she said she had such positive
knowledge of things; to which she replied that she got it from her brother,
who had been shut up in the prison,
and therefore knew all about it. I
quietly interviewed this brother, who
seemed a remarkably healthy, jovial
sort of fellow, and he privately acknowledged to me that he had manufactured all these stories to make
himself out a martyr and a hero in
the eyes of the young girls of the village. He told me that there were a
number of young men in town who
had a good deal of money which their
fathers had made by being sutlers
and camp-followers, and, as he didn't
have much money himself, he determined to outshine them by trumpet-
ing up a military glory. As he was a
clever sort of fellow, whenever his em-

bellishment of a story was such that my conscience would allow, I corroborated him, so that between us we routed the sutlers completely, and I had the satisfaction of seeing him marry the nicest and best girl in the town. His wife never could understand why it was that her husband appeared now to like me rather than otherwise, when only a short time ago we had been shooting at each other.

"Another authority on Libby Prison matters, responsible for many of these stories, and a person who has made considerable money out of them, is an old colored porter, whom the proprietors of the fertilizer works employed about the premises. He was a remarkably shrewd negro, and could tell a person's position in life with great precision. He was in the habit of keeping a number of old bullets, musket-balls, locks, and such things on hand, which he constantly replenished from a neighboring junk shop. These he would sell to visitors and tourists, accompanying each with a plausible story of some sort or other. Among these I recollect an amusing occurrence between him and an elderly lady with spectacles on. I was in the office talking with one of the clerks, when she drove up in a carriage. The clerk winked at the porter and told him there was another chance. The cunning old fellow put on a look that would have done credit to his brother preacher when he gives out his text, 'the sun do move,' and asked the old lady if he could do anything for her. As she wanted to see the prison, he said he could show her around, and as he came into the office for his hat said, 'Marse Reg., she am a schoolmarm; I'se got a bran-new 'count for her.' With this he went off, and was gone some time. When they got back I noticed a hard-set expression upon the

old lady's face, and that the darkey
could hardly keep quiet. As soon as
she was out of hearing he said: '''Fore
de Lord, Marse Reg., how I dun fool
dat white lady.' When asked to explain, he said that when they came to
the hole in the wall, through which
the prisoners had escaped, he told her
all about it; then went on to say that
the next morning after the escape the
authorities had locked the prisoners'
legs together, two by two, so that
they could no longer get out, and that
he had hid away one of the very locks
that had been used for that purpose.
After bargaining around for a little
while, he said that she finally gave
him *that* for the old lock, and with
this he flourished a new five-dollar
note. I was so impressed with the
scene, and with the mischief that might
be spread abroad by such nonsense,
that I went to the officers of the company and remonstrated against their

allowing it. They seemed to regard
the whole matter as a joke, and would
not interfere. At the same time they
told me that I would be surprised at
the gullibility which many travellers
exhibited about this building, who in
other matters were sensible people."

As they drove away from the scene
Edyth heard the hum of machinery
and the sound of many voices singing
in a neighboring factory—a fitting end
to so many discordant elements.

They next ascended a high hill, from
which a most magnificent view was
obtained. Colonel Carter rested his
horses here, while he described the different points of interest which were
spread out as in a panorama before
them. On their right lay the city of
Richmond, with its prominent buildings, and its church spires rearing aloft
against the sky their sun-lit points, like
so many islands in an ocean's waste.
On yonder hill had perched the raven,

croaking his midnight dirges for the
lost Lenore. There lay Belle Isle, another of those beautiful oases amidst
the desert of smoky industry. The
city of Manchester was before them,
wedded to the river as the city of the
Lombards was to the Adriatic. Far
off towards the south could be seen
the majestic river, on its way to the
sea. Its giant strength was harnessed. The low-lying walls and the
terraces could readily be traced, and
where the hand of man had been laid
upon the river's mane, the mighty current was doing its appointed task.
The river was deepening itself. On a
neighboring hill was disclosed one of
the resting-places of the old Indian
warrior, since made into a home for
the white man. The stone around
which the savage orgies had been en-
acted was surrounded by a vine; the
hush of silence reigned o'er Pow-
hatan's grave. The horizon's edge

was touched at the point where once
the fierce conflict of two armed hosts
had fought out the first of modern
battles between the land and the sea.
The silent river was flowing beneath
them, but what memories were voiced
up from its hollow tones! Its mouth
had beheld the cradle of our race.
Two great wars, that marked a new
era upon the world, were fought along
its shores; while the siege of York-
town and the fall of Richmond settled
the destinies of mankind within sight
of its waters. Upon its bosom were
borne the fourths as tribute to the
English king. Near to its end took
place the first great struggle between
iron-clad foes. An Indian chief, when
pursued by vindictive assailants,
found friendly rescue upon its tide. A
hostile army, such as the world has
rarely surpassed, was saved from destruction when sheltered by its embrace.

As Colonel Carter drew these pictures of a vanished age his voice sounded like that of Monker waking up the dead. Edyth could see in fancy the different scenes on which he touched. There was Newport, bringing succor and great help to the ill-fated colonists. There was the low-lying Monitor and her great antagonist locked in their giant contest, while the solitary tower at Jamestown was telling of a time that had flown. The armies of Cornwallis and of McClellan were before her vision, and the thunder of the Galena's guns seemed to echo in her ears. To her it was the imagery of language, but to him it was the resurrection of the past.

As silence ensued he broke it through by saying that he would now drive her to some of the breastworks around Richmond, and accordingly directed his horses towards the

Osborne pike.   When they came upon
the open road he asked her if she
would be afraid to have the horses
put to their highest speed.   On receiving her assent he nodded to the
groom, who, immediately unfolded
his arms and took hold of the sup-
ports; then he spoke to the horses.
At the first sound of his voice the
noble animals pricked up their ears
and started.   Three times, in rapid
succession, he shouted into their ears
the word of command, and at each
time they responded by increasing
their speed; at the last they rushed
forward in a headlong gait, while the
foam flew from their mouths; objects
began now to go by like spectres in a
dream, fire flashed from the wheels,
and the wind whistled as they went
along.   Suddenly she heard an un-
earthly screech, and at the same time
Colonel Carter ejaculated Merciful
Father.   Looking ahead she saw a

little child tottering directly in their way. In an instant the horses came upon it; she could see the innocent smile of delight as, unconscious of danger, it stood directly in the path. A choking sensation came upon her; she could hardly breathe; she caught hold of Colonel Carter's arm, but it was as rigid as steel as he guided the horses; then suddenly all consciousness ceased. A sudden thrill went through her. Her lips felt a sensation so unusual that it sent the life-blood back through her veins. She opened her eyes slowly, as consciousness returned, and saw Colonel Carter bending over her.

"What is the matter?" she exclaimed, and then, as the recollection of the occurrence returned, she asked if the child was killed.

"Not even scratched," Colonel Carter replied thankfully. "I reined the horses so that the child passed in

between them, and was not harmed
at all. I would never have forgiven
myself had it been hurt."

As she sat upright, freeing herself
from Colonel Carter's support, she
caught a glimpse of the tiger's face.
His arms were folded rigidly as before,
his eyes looked dead ahead, but they
now shone with a light that was almost unreal. Divining her thought,
Colonel Carter said, "You need not
mind him; he can neither hear nor
speak. What he sees is as it were
buried in a grave."

By this time they were well on the
way to Warwick Park, where the in-
nermost line of defences was built, and
where a remnant of the Confederate
army crossed the James when Richmond fell into the hands of its vic-
torious foe. As they drove down the
beautiful road, which, winding around,
leads by a gentle descent from the hills
to the plain, an overpowering sense

of sadness came over him. He told
her of that morning, many years ago,
when on a day although as joyous
as this with nature's outbursts, yet
he had come down that very road
with as heavy a heart as a man could
bear with his few surviving comrades.
He told her how they had fought to
save the city; how, night after night
during the long winter hours, they
had slept in the trenches, momentarily
expecting a foe overwhelming in numbers; how, though time after time
they had repulsed the enemy, slaugh-
tering them almost like cattle, yet fresh
numbers seemed always springing up,
while when they lost a comrade there
was none to replace him. He told her
how awful was his realization that
finally they must yield, but how he
struggled against this feeling, for fear
of discouraging the others; how the
Great Chieftain would go down the
line; how undaunted he bore himself

before his men, while his heart was breaking within its secret recesses. Finally, when the supreme moment had come, and they knew that all was lost, they retreated down this very road, and took a last look upon the devoted city as they crossed the river. He paused; although nearly a quarter of a century had elapsed since that day, the memory of it overcame him even now, and he averted his face that his companion might not see the emotion which he could not control.

As Edyth realized that she was being shown some of the most sacred and lofty feelings of his life, a great compassion overcame her. Holding out her hand to him, she said:

"Colonel Carter, I often did you and your countrymen a great wrong in my imagination. I am heartily sorry for it now, and ask your and their forgiveness."

Tenderly taking her hand, he raised

it to his lips, while his countenance expressed that which made language unnecessary. The tiger's arms were folded tighter than ever before, his eyes again became luminous, but their gaze was directed skyward.

CHAPTER VI.

THE HUGUENOT.

The next morning broke gloomily.
As if to make amends for the pleasant
sunshine of the past, clouds now over-
spread the heavens, and the rain came
in torrents upon the earth.   When
Edyth awoke, a feeling of foreboding
was upon her.   As she descended to
the breakfast-table it increased, and
it did not need the lowering clouds to
intensify her depression.   A note was
handed her as she sat down.   It only
required a glance to tell her from
whom it came.   Its contents read as
follows:

"*Dear Miss Prescott :*

"Were it not presumptuous in me
to call to my aid the author of Lalla

Rookh, I would fain borrow his language to express my regret at parting from you once more. This evening I was requested to meet certain investors, who are desirous of looking into some of our enterprises. They have arranged to leave the city by the early train to-morrow, and it is imperative that I should accompany them. I will therefore be compelled to leave without seeing you again. Were the affair one of my own, I might be tempted to disregard the summons; but as the property of other parties, who have trusted me in these matters, is under discussion, it would not be right for me to neglect their interests. Accordingly I must delegate to my pen what I would prefer to lighten by utterance of my tongue, and that is a farewell. I know of no better way of signing myself than as

"Yours,

"RANDOLPH CARTER."

Why was it that a sudden dimness
seemed to grow up before her, or why
this feeling of melancholy? Was it
the dismal rain which .affected her,
and had some dark cloud obscured
the rays of the sun already hidden?
Her father joined her presently with
his morning paper, but she felt no
inclination to interrupt him in his
reading. Her appetite was gone, and
she listlessly waited for the meal to
be over. Her father read from the
paper a list of names which at first
were unmeaning to her; but a sudden
interest in them arose when the paper
went on to state that the parties
mentioned were investigating invest-
ments in Virginia, and had left that
morning on the early train, accompanied by local promoters. Among
these Colonel Carter was mentioned,
evidently as one of the important
members. After her father had
finished reading the paper she asked

him for it and took it to her room,
when he, bidding her good-by, had
gone to the club to find there a solace
and amusement which is denied to a
woman. At home she had been accustomed to being left alone, and had
not found it irksome, because there
was so much to do. But here it was
different. There was nothing for her
to do. The rain came down too
mercilessly for her to go out with
comfort. So she staid in her room,
and her mind, having nothing else to
feed upon, dwelt in imagination upon
the scenes she had recently gone
through. She read and re-read his
letter. There was no clue to where
he had gone, or when he would return. If he returned and did not
come to see her, what then? She
would banish his image from her
recollection, cost what it might.
Suppose she and her father left the
city before he returned. There was

the doubt. Would he follow her and
press the advantage that he had
gained? Would he know where to
follow? There was no indication in
his letter of a desire to know where
she was going. Then suddenly there
came ringing upon her senses the old
song, "tender and true," "forever
true."

"Come what will, I will not doubt
him," she said to herself, and then
went down to the drawing-room to
escape from her own thoughts.

The afternoon mail brought a letter from her aunt, Mrs. Pickney, saying that she and her daughter Maud
would join them, and as the letter
was delayed by a storm at the North,
of which the rain in Richmond was a
part, the date of their arrival in Richmond was that very evening. They
arrived on time.

Mrs. Pickney was tired out by the
journey, having come through from

New York without change of cars, and
accordingly she immediately retired,
leaving Edyth and Maud to entertain
one another.

Maud Pickney was a great contrast to her cousin. The fortune, or,
better, the misfortune, of good looks
had been denied her; but she was
worth her weight in gold, as her
younger brother expressed it, when,
having. plunged into some extrava-
gances from which he had been unable
to extricate himself without appeal to
the paternal assistance, he told her
his troubles. She not only sympa-
thized with him, but unselfishly gave
him enough of her scanty savings
to tide over the pressing emergency.
She was as full of fun as she was
meagre in looks, and at school she
could at any time upset the gravity
of the class-room by one of her sallies
of wit. She was a great tease, and
would laugh out of an eccentricity or

folly those whom she could reach in no
other way. She was a little older
than Edyth, and hence always assumed a sort of motherly attitude towards her, yet at the same time there
was the greatest cordiality between
the two. Edyth, however, was afraid
of her ridicule, nor did she dare to
tell her what was uppermost in her
thoughts. Her quick-witted cousin
was too keen not to detect that her
gayety was assumed—that something
was forced in her manner, and that
Edyth was not the same that she had
been in Boston. She was determined
to find out what it was, so, when
Edyth least expected such a thing, she
exclaimed:

"Out with it, Edyth. Has some
negro fetish-worshipper horrified you
into dumbness, or has some rebel
brigadier made a raid into your affec-
tions and gone off, leaving desolation
behind?"

With this the merry girl broke into a hearty laugh, as the absurdity of the idea of her cold and haughty cousin being at all interested in such an uncanny admirer in so short a time. "Great Cæsar's ghost *rem acu tetigi*," she continued, as a glance at her cousin's face told her how true a mark this random shaft had hit.

This had come so suddenly upon Edyth that she had not had time to prepare. The unbidden blood mounted to her cheeks and set her face aglow. She stood betrayed.

Her cousin advanced towards her, and, raising her finger, as if in reprimand, in a tone of mock solemnity, said: "Edyth, it is not possible that you have allowed a rebel brigadier, in one short week, to capture what others have so far only been able to besiege."

As Edyth kept silent, she continued: "Has he a Rosinante? Where is his

Sancho Panza? Bring him forth, that
I may annihilate him with a word."
And again the merry girl broke out
into a silvery laugh at the idea and
the sight of her cousin's confusion.

As banter such as this only caused
Edyth to keep silence, her cousin essayed a different tactic. Again keeping up her mockery, but at the same
time putting a pathos into her voice
that was almost real, she said,

"Come, rest on my bosom, my own stricken dear;
　If he has deserted thee, I am still here;"

and with this she playfully forced
Edyth's head down upon her breast.
Her surprise was intense when, on her
cousin's head touching her, she detected a smothered sob.

That night Edyth could not sleep.
As often as her senses began to fall
away, and it seemed as if she might
lose all consciousness in repose, a
vivid recollection would spring up.

Gone, then, was unconsciousness and rest, and in its place came thought intense, with recollection and with pain. The long and weary hours crept slowly by, their passage marked by the striking of a neighboring bell. Many such nights, she recalled, had Colonel Carter passed beneath an uncovered roof, in front of an advancing foe. The air of angry winter roared around. It found her sheltered and wrapped up in clothes. Him it had discovered exposed, with only his martial cloak around him. Her senses passed to those of an unsubstantial dream. Before her eyes he appeared asleep upon his couch; the solitary sentry's back was turned, while from behind came up a spectral host, about to overwhelm him. "Save him!" she cried, and with this awoke, to find herself kneeling upright, with outstretched arms, suppliant to the empty air.

The day now began to break. A

sudden gleam shot over the sky, as if
a ray of light had pierced through
the mist-laden air. A roseate hue
began to tinge the clouds, and the
morning star commenced to pale.
The heavy rain had ceased and the
leaden clouds were breaking away in
the east. The rosy lining to the
clouds spread abroad; they began to
reflect to the earth the rays of the
rising sun; inanimate nature appeared, as it were, to awake; and
the early chanticleer gave out his
morning song. As a low-lying cloud
cleared away, the top of a high
church-steeple was bathed in light.
It descended down the spire. The
tops of the lofty buildings now caught
the rays, and soon the limb of the sun
himself appeared, ushering in the new-
born day. She dropped into a deep
sleep. The ethereal light had dispelled
her gloom, and she slept, quiet as a
child. The day had far advanced

when she descended to the breakfast-
table. All had finished, and she was
left to partake of her meal alone.
Her spirits had recovered their tone.
With the elasticity of youth she had
put her sorrow behind her, as the
swing of the pendulum that turned
from the gloom of night to the joy of
day.

Her father proposed that they all
take a drive, and shortly afterwards
she found herself again before Libby
Prison. To her it was an old story
now. She listened incredulously to
the tale of the porter, as he, discern-
ing Mr. Prescott's weak point, dwelt
upon the starvation of the prisoners.
Her aunt's woman's sympathy was
aroused, and together she and Mr.
Prescott soundly berated the Southern authorities. This began to make
Edyth indignant, but she bridled her
tongue. Finally, however, when they
had all seated themselves in the carriage, and were about to drive away,

Mr. Prescott's last straw broke the camel's back, as he said what a burning shame it had been that the prisoners should have been allowed to suffer so for food in that land of plenty. Edyth could stand it no longer.

"I do not believe a word of it," she said, "or, if food was scarce, it was because it was not to be obtained. I have it on the best authority that the food served the prisoners in that prison was the same as that furnished the Southern troops in the field. I can never be made to believe that a nation as brave and chivalrous as this would have maltreated helpless prisoners, or one so proverbial for hospitality would have denied them food were it at hand."

It was bravely spoken. She was astonished at her own temerity, after it was said; but she had thrown down the gauntlet and was ready to champion the Southern cause.

Mrs. Pickney, for the first time in

her life, did a thing she would have considered abhorrent in others. She dropped her lower jaw, and, with mouth wide open, gazed at her niece in speechless astonishment. Mr. Prescott was aroused entirely out of his usual complacency, and demanded of his daughter who was her authority for such statements. Maud gave a low whistle, (which accomplishment she had learned after great difficulty,) and, pinching Edyth underneath the carriage-covers, asked in a whisper where was the rebel brigadier.

They also drove to Marshall Park, and out upon the crest of that same hill where only a short time before Edyth and Colonel Carter had visited. The beauty of the scene aroused the slumbering eloquence of the dusky charioteer, who in his turn essayed to describe the surroundings. Addressing Mr. Prescott as the head of the party, he said:

"Dat, sar, whar you sees de flag pol' on de ruf' ob dat house, am Gamble's Hill. Dat is whar de yun bucks and de gals takes demselbes on Sunday nites. In de day-time de peple from de Norf dey drives out dar to see de scen'ry. Rite below de hill am whar dey used ter make cannons and big guns endurin' ob de war. Dat smoke dar, de oder side ob dat bridge, am Belle Isle. Dat is whar dey had more prisoners. Dey makes nales an hors' shues dar now. Ober the riber, dat am Manchester. I calls de peple dat cums from dar, hoodoos! Below dar am Jeemes's ribber. It am a fine, large stream. De ole Injuns used ter bake the hoe-cake an dance deselves down yarnder whar you sees dat house in de trees. Dat am whar dey says de ole King Pow'tan am buried. Dat used to be de hom' ob one ob de ole families of Virginny. Dat is whar General Wingfield Scott fund his wif.

Way ober dar, just so fur as you can see, dat am Drewry's Bluff. 'Fore de Lord! how many ded fokes I seed dere one day. I was in dat fite, sar." Here the old fellow straightened himself up, as a recollection of his martial days returned to him, and he became quite loquacious as he saw what an interested audience he had. "Yer see, sar, I had a 'sponsible duty dat day. I was on de general's staff, and had ter do 'cordin. I was in charge ob de kulnary apartment."

"You mean you were chief cook and bottle-washer," Maud mischievously explained.

"Dat, marm, am anudder way ob 'pressin' it; but I dunt think it gibes nuf 'portance to what I dun. You sees, I wuz jist gitting de corn-bred reddy 'fore de brake of day, fur dat was all we had den, when rip, whir, bang, and afore I cud say Jack Robinson I seed de blue coats a comin'. It

wuz a foggy mornin', and dey cum up
fore we wus ware of it. I made dub-
ble-quick time to the rear, to bring up
reinforcements, and I staid dar all dat
day to see dat dey wus bein' refreshed."

"You don't mean to say, Kinchen,"
Mr. Prescott enquired with much
curiosity, "that you were with the
Southern troops that day, and having an opportunity to escape, did not
join your liberators."

"If you mean by dat, sar, dat I
'serted ter de Yankees, I tells you no
sar! I fullud my young massa fur
three yers, and when, sar, de bullet
hit him abuv his hart an he lay down
ter die, I marked de place, and dat
nite, when de soldiers was retreatin',
I crep' inside de lines and I kivered up
his body, whar it lay until de war
was ober; den dey tuk it home and
buried it 'longside de soldiers dat was
wid him."

The faithful old negro here looked

furtively around, to see that no one was in hearing; then continued: "When de lectshun-time cumes round I allers votes as de 'publicans says, but when I gits into trubbles I goes ter my old Massa's family an dey helps me out."

To Mr. Prescott it came like a revelation—this phase of the war. There was, then, no doubt but that there had been innumerable instances, where the negroes could have joined the Northern armies, but had voluntarily remained with their old masters. But it was with a feeling of intense relief, he reflected that the question of slavery had been settled forever. Its passions, its pathos, and its power, alike are gone. The devotedness of that race has found few parallels in history. It is well that it should have received so able a tribute as that given by the rising novelist, whose facile pen has so eloquently described such scenes in Marse Chan.

During the remainder of the drive
a constraining silence rested upon all.
Edyth could not but contrast it with
her former drive. The same scene
was there, the same sky, but he who
had lent such life to all this scene was
away. Maud was now thoroughly
convinced that she had discovered
Edyth's secret, and was on the *qui
vive* to determine the one particular
brigadier, Mrs. Pickney was trying
to solve the problem of Edyth's par-
tisanship, while Mr. Prescott had re-
lapsed into reveries of the past.

That night a council was held to
determine whither they should next
direct their journey. Mrs. Pickney
was for getting Edyth away from
Richmond, but was afraid of Florida
on account of the rapidly returning
warm weather there. Mr. Prescott
did not wish to be too far away from
the club and the morning papers.
Edyth took no part in the discussion;
so Maud, as was usual with her,

decided the question for the entire
party. She had heard of a place
called the Huguenot Springs, that
was just being reopened and brought
into prominence again after an eclipse
of thirty years' duration. At one
time it had beheld the wealth and
fashion of Virginia as guests within
its domains. When the iron hoof of
war came upon the land it was
devoted to the use of the invalid
soldiers. On the restoration of peace
it had passed through many vicissitudes, until finally it had found pur-
chasers from the North, attracted by
the fame of its waters. These were of
undoubted merit, while the sulphur
spring was specially noted for its
effect in restoring enfeebled powers.
There was something of romance connected with the name, there is much
of beauty inherent in the place, and
Maud rightly inferred that, having
passed into the possession of energetic

proprietors, it would early recover its ancient glory. It was accordingly decided that they go to the Huguenot Springs.

The next morning found them on their way up the Alleghany railroad. The scenery along the route was so totally different from what they had imagined it would be, that it even aroused the unpoetical Mrs. Pickney into admiration. The graceful curves of the river, the ruggedness of the cliffs, and the fertility of the lowlands, were well worthy her praise.

Arrived at the station, they made their first acquaintance with a typical southern scene. There was the wide and shallow ferry-boat, with its dusky ferryman. The river lazily rolled the water along, the current being stilled for several miles by the dam, which, obstructing its flow, directed a portion of its life-giving stream to the thirsty city below.

Behind them were the high, rocky cliffs, while in front was the river. Maud was enthusiastic over the scene. She put at once an embargo upon such similes as Washington crossing the Delaware, or Charon ferrying the Styx, but broke out herself into the refrain of the Danube river, as the boatman, loosening the chain, shoved out into the stream. On the other side of the river stages awaited them, and they were soon on the way to the hotel. The climb was gradual, so that they did not notice their elevation until, coming upon the long boulevard, the unobstructed view was before them. The time-honored oaks, with their spreading branches, the rolling landscape, and the hills across the river formed a picture which was itself a dream.

Mr. Prescott secured a private parlor for the use of his party, and rooms adjoining, then gave himself up to the pleasures of his surround-

ings; for it was pleasant to a gentleman to be environed with comfort
and ease, and look out upon the
world from such quarters. There was
no lack of visitors, but these were
almost entirely composed of members
of the softer sex. They had therefore
invaded the domain of the gentlemen
and monopolized the billiard-rooms,
and other quarters usually denied
them.

When the two cousins parted for
the night, Maud said: "Edyth, if
your rebel brigadier follows you into
this woman-ridden place, I give you
fair warning that I will set the dogs
upon him. I cannot stand by and see
so much humanity suffering, and you
alone revelling in this love-inspiring
abode."

With this playful threat she kissed
her cousin good-night and left her
dreaming of the unknown future.
How little did either of them antici-
pate the terrible reality before them!

CHAPTER VII.

THE GAME OF CHESS.

Time was passing. Already the mild effulgence of the sun had betokened that spring was indeed come and well upon them. A fortnight had elapsed, and over the length and breadth of the land a new life was springing up. The fields were putting forth their increase, the wanton lapwing was getting himself another crest, and all animate nature was holding a high carnival of love. Maud was ever on the watch for the disturbing element of Edyth's dreams, but no one had as yet appeared whom she could select as the one.

Edyth and she had become quite fond of billiards, and they often

amused themselves in that way, either
together or as partners in a four-
handed game.   One evening they were
playing a many-sided game, when the
sound of several voices, issuing from
the adjoining room, (a room that had
been partitioned off from the billiard-
tables, and which was now the bar-
room,) proclaimed an addition to the
guests. The new-comers were evidently welcomed, and such exclama-
tions as old fellow, old man, and other
epithets, which indicate a feeling of
cordiality, were rapidly exchanged.
Maud, who was sitting near the door,
was surprised to hear her uncle's voice
among the rest as welcoming the new
arrivals, and began wondering who
they could be.   She solved the problem
to her satisfaction by putting it down
that some Bostonians had arrived,
and made her shot with as much non-
chalance as if she was not burning
with curiosity to hear their names.

A momentary silence fell upon the group, which she correctly interpreted as that during which the glasses were being filled; then she heard a voice distinctly say: "Gentlemen, I give you greeting. Mr. Prescott, I drink to your good health," and with this there was a jingling of glasses and another ominous silence, and then a succession of raps as the glasses were put down on the counter.

But what was the matter with Edyth? She missed a dead shot and ignominiously pocketed her ball in the corner-pocket, while a tell-tale color began stealing over her face.

Maud had not long to wait for an explanation. Again she heard that same voice say, "I will accompany you, then, and pay my respects to the ladies now."

The door opened and a gentleman entered along with Mr. Prescott. His piercing eyes rapidly scanned the faces

of those present. When his gaze met
Edyth's they flashed; a sudden light
seemed to spring from their depths,
and his beautiful smile illumined his
entire countenance. His pace quickened, and he stood beside her; then he
spoke to her in a tone too subdued for
others to hear. Maud was hastened
by these proceedings into what to her
was an unpardonable sin—a gram-
matical error. "That's him; I'll bet
a copper denarius that's him," she
ejaculated to herself when she saw the
meeting between the two.

He turned with Mr. Prescott, and
was introduced to her mother; then
to herself.

During all this time Maud could
not but admire the self-possession of
the man, and his perfect bearing, as he
acknowledged each introduction by
something appropriate to each acquaintance. He would not allow the
game of billiards to be interrupted,

but sat down by Mrs. Pickney, and in a few well-chosen words ingratiated himself once and for all in that worthy lady's estimation.

Edyth saw that Maud was watching her like a lynx, while every now and then she felt there was another gaze upon her, from which she longed to escape. She missed carom after carom, until her cousin became completely exasperated.

"Edyth," she finally exclaimed, "I must disown you. You disgrace our side so that I am going to turn you out and get a better partner. Go! Play a game of euchre, or, better yet, a game of chess, where you can immolate some victim on the altar of your scientific play, for I'll give you credit for skill at that; but billiards to-night is not your forte."

"If Miss Prescott will accept such an offering, I present myself as a victim, to be sacrificed on the altar of her science," Colonel Carter immediately said, as he saw his opportunity of separating Edyth from the others.

"Go, Edyth," Maud replied, before she had a chance to speak, "and beat him. Redeem yourself and win such a wager as shall make amends for your losses here"; for she was amused at the quickness with which Colonel Carter seized hold of his opportunity, and she determined to help him on.

Edyth obeyed mechanically, and led the way to their parlor, leaving the others to finish their game. She brought out the chess-men, and once more waited for him to speak.

"Your cousin has imposed an unfair task on me, in that she has matched your scientific skill against my untrained thought. What wager will you make as forfeit in case I win and do not fall a victim to your power?"

"What wager do you want?" she

innocently inquired; for, being a fine player, she did not doubt but that she would readily win.

"Your lips," Colonel Carter instantly replied.

"How dare you speak to me like that?" the high-spirited girl indignantly asked, as she felt, for the first time, the assertion of a lover's claim.

Like as a high-mettled steed frets and grows restive under the rein, so she rebelled against this restraint. Had Colonel Carter quailed or shown the slightest sign of being dismayed, he would have sunk forever in her estimation, and experienced her scorn; but he had now too much at stake to be so easily repelled.

"The men of my race dare anything," he said, "when the prize is a magnificent woman like yourself. I am determined to win your heart and hand; your lips are but the highway to them. You have matched your intellect against mine; let the wager be as I have said it, and I would stake my greatest possession in forfeit for it."

He had cast the die. He now waited for her reply, looking at her outwardly as steadily as he had faced the great crises of his life before, and as collectedly; but inwardly, he trembled to think that his whole after career in life hung by the thread of her answer.

"But you have no stake commensurate with mine," she answered in argument.

She had hesitated. To hesitate was to lose, for, once admitted to argument, the victory was his.

"Make my forfeit anything you please," he continued, "so long as you give me but the chance to win. I will accept and bide the issue by it."

"But you have nothing that I desire," she replied; "moreover, you

would think my conduct light were I
to play for such a wager."

"Now, by high heaven I swear
that if my unruly tongue should ever
say a word which was unkind
towards you, or an unbidden thought
arise, which linked with indiscretion
your fair name, I would uproot it
from its very hold and cast it from
me."

He spoke this rapidly and vehe-
mently at first, then passionately, as
he protested against her imaginary
accusation; he softened his voice
towards the last, and ended with
that silvery cadence of his tongue
which carried such resolution in its
tone.

"Hush," she said in a low voice.
"Do not swear. Man's asseveration
should be such as not to need an oath
to prove it."

A pause ensued. She had dropped
her eyes away from his, and as she

finished speaking she began to twist the chessmen unmeaningly in her hand. At last she arranged them in consecutive order, and without uttering a word moved a pawn. Colonel Carter quietly took his seat, and moved the corresponding pawn to his king's fourth square. She next moved her king's bishop's pawn to the fourth square, thus paving the way to a brilliant opening. Colonel Carter declined the gambit pawn, and moved his queen's pawn to her fourth square.

"Oh, you coward," Edyth exclaimed, as this move, although the strongest that could be made, prevented the brilliant combination made possible by her opening.

"If you will allow it, I will withdraw that move and take the gambit pawn instead," and without waiting for an answer, he made the exchange. Edyth immediately replied by moving the king's knight to pre-

THE HUGUENOT LOVERS.   169

vent a possible check to her king, and
Colonel Carter pushed his king's
knight's pawn to its fourth square in
order to maintain his forward pawn.
Edyth next moved her king's bishop
to the queen bishop's fourth square,
so as to attack Colonel Carter's exposed king, while he replied by advancing his pawn to attack her knight.
Edyth then castled, and although by
so doing she sacrificed a knight, yet
she gained a position of such advantage that it is considered by some to
be almost overwhelming.   Colonel
Carter promptly took the knight with
his pawn, and the game was opened
in earnest.   Soon afterwards Mrs.
Pickney came in the parlor to play
propriety, but as the game was perfectly silent and uninviting to lookers-
on, and moreover, as she was made
drowsy by the warm rooms, she soon
retired.   Mr. Prescott was too absent-
minded to do more than make a pass-
. 8

ing salutation as he went along; and
the game slowly proceeded, as each
one carefully considered the other's
move. Later Maud came in and
looked at both of them. They were
so absorbed in the game as to pay but
slight attention to her.

As she was about to go she said:
"Colonel Carter, I am going to do to
Edyth as the darkeys say; I am going
to 'conjur' her, so that you can beat
her"; and with this she made some
fanciful gesticulations in the air, then,
suddenly stooping down, she whispered in her ear, "Edyth, I think your
brigadier is just splendid"; after
which she solemnly walked away, telling Col. Carter that it was all right
now; that she had put Edyth under a
spell, and that he would certainly win.
She then made a sweeping curtsey
and declaimed, "I'd say good-night
till it be morrow." With that she retired. Her cousin's playful attitude

and whispered remark distracted Edyth's attention from the game. She exposed a piece, by which Colonel Carter was able to make an exchange, and although the exchange was even, yet it weakened her attack. Finally her attack lost its force and passed to Colonel Carter's side. He took advantage of it at once. She could not prevent an exchange, and he forced one at every chance. Although she maintained the exchanges even, still the loss of the knight, sacrificed in the beginning in order to get a good position, was being felt. Finally, the game was reduced down to a contest with pawns. Colonel Carter made a strategic sacrifice of his knight for a pawn, and by this move was able to push a pawn to the eighth square, thus winning a queen.

He then said, "Are you willing to confess that the game is now mine?"

To which Edyth merely replied, "Yes."

"Was it fairly won?" was his next inquiry; to which again she merely answered "yes."

With this he arose and went up to her and asked, "What have you to say why you should not now pay your forfeit?" and as he said these words he gently took her hand, while a great light leaped up into his eyes, and his countenance thoroughly expressed the anticipation that was before him. As his intention became apparent to her, she drew away her hand, and moved backwards with a gesture as of repulsion.

When Colonel Carter perceived this, the bright look faded from his countenance, and he haughtily drew himself up to his full height as he said, "I am too proud to claim that which is so distasteful to you to confer. You need not be afraid that I would force an unwelcome caress upon you. I will be sufficiently generous to release you from a debt which seems so repugnant to you to pay."

The clock struck twelve. He bowed as if to bid her good-night, but she had no idea of letting him go until he became submissive to her woman's power. Looking up at him half tenderly, half reproachfully, she said in a voice so low that he had to bend his head in order to catch the words: "It was the idea, and not the man, that was repugnant to me."

CHAPTER VIII.

WHAT IS LOVE?

A great gayety now set in at the Huguenot. There were arrivals from the far South, fleeing from the approaching warmth of the summer sun, and travellers from the distant North, escaping from the chill of the winter wind. Many from the neighboring country also came flocking in to see the visitors that were already there. Among these was Colonel Carter's elder brother, Peyton. The brothers were astonishingly alike in appearance, but far different in disposition and affairs. Peyton Carter had also been a colonel in the Confederate army At the end of the war he turned his attention to farm-

ing, but for many years had found it
difficult to make both ends meet. Of
late years his circumstances had been
somewhat easier, and he devoted
what leisure time he had to travel,
and in this way enlarged his ideas
of men and things far beyond his
early opportunities. He was even
more courtly in his bearing and manner than his brother Randolph, and
as great a favorite with ladies, but
not so well used to the business
requirements and methods of the
present day. He was one of the last
remaining gentlemen of the old school,
that is now so rapidly passing away,
and was somewhat irrelevantly styled
the "Last of the Mohicans" by the
young leaders of the new society. It
would have done one good to have
witnessed the meeting of the two
brothers. There was the cordial
grasp of the hand and smile of greeting The words were few, but their
meaning was pregnant. At last Ran-

dolph Carter asked his brother what brought him there.

"Well, Randolph," he replied, "I thought I would run over for a few days and renew some of my old acquaintances; you know it is very lonesome on a plantation by yourself, and there may be some one here that would make it a little less solitary;" and with that he smiled a most knowing smile at this idea of his getting married—a thing a man who is a confirmed bachelor is always hinting at but never doing.

"Old fellow, if that is what you are up to, you must rejuvenate. These young fellows that are coming on will put an old stager, like yourself, entirely in the back-ground. You had better drink some of these waters and see if they will not realize the dream of Ponce de Leon, and give you a new lease on youth," Randolph facetiously replied.

"If I thought it would do me any good," Peyton responded, "I should drink a pitcherful each day."

"You had better drink a barrelful," Randolph advised, for it was well known to him that his brother had frolicked a great deal as a young man, and now was feeling the effects of it.

While this conversation was taking place between the brothers, a new guest arrived at the hotel, whose influence upon the after lives of both of them was very great, but of which they were at present entirely unconscious. It is needless to say to one who knew the character of each, that this person was a woman, and a beautiful one at that. She was now a widow, having lost her husband two years before—a man many years her senior, who left her a large estate, and, what is rare in such cases, free to do with it as she chose.

Mr. Arlington, for such was the

name of the widow's husband, was a
self-made man. He knew nothing of
his own parentage, and had no
relatives to contest his will. As an
office-boy he had made a start in life in
a western city, and, having emigrated
to the Pacific coast, had accumulated
there a fortune. By accident he
drifted to the coal and oil region of
Pennsylvania, and, having some spare
capital to invest, again found fortune
favoring him. Doubling his invest-
ments in the oil regions, he withdrew
from business and settled down in
Boston, to enjoy in his declining
years the wealth that he had made.
He had heard of the culture of that
city, and of the fame of the univer-
sity so closely allied to it, and he
imagined that a residence in such an
environment would have its reflex
influence upon himself. He had bought
a house; the world said he had
bought his wife; but that was a cruel

slander on the young girl that he led
as a bride to the altar, for she had
deliberately chosen him, in preference
to more congenial suitors. That his
money had influenced her decision she
never denied; that this money should
bring her consolation and comfort he
had ever desired. She had done her
part nobly by him. She had no father
or mother living, they having died
when she was a child; but her grandparents, with whom she lived, were
of ancient descent. They were poor,
but so well connected that the grand-
child had the *entre* to many houses
closed to persons of greater worldly
possessions but less distinguished
lineage. On her marriage she took
her husband with her. At first people laughed at him, but endured him
for her sake; soon his solid worth
won its way, and he was welcomed
on his own account, and he learned
by absorption. His wife had made

him a position in that social world;
he had kept it. He had loved her
with his whole soul; she had respected
him; and when his last great hour
had come upon earth, and, dismissing
all others, he told her how she had
brightened the declining years of his
life, she had wept to think that she
had not done a greater part by him.
Gently soothing her, he bade her farewell and surrendered his soul to its
Great Creator with a blessing upon
her head. She had mourned for him
truly, but now she was free—free as a
bird, to come and go. She had done
her duty by him while he lived; but
now she had no duty. There could
be no congeniality between May and
December. It is an outrage on great
Nature's laws, and she had suffered
by violating them; but now December
had gone away, and a glorious sum-
mer-time was before her. At first she
plunged into an excess of freedom;

but she soon became harassed by lack of experience. She was a victim of ceaseless importunities on all sides; nor did she have any real true friend to whom she could apply for advice. Her latest idea was to travel in a yacht. This, too, had given her unending trouble and annoyance; so she had left the yacht anchored in the river at Richmond, and had come to the Huguenot for a little rest and quiet. At once she became a great favorite at the hotel, for she had a true heart, and never allowed herself to speak ill of any one; and her fortune made her the object of attraction, both to sycophants and friends.

Both Edyth and Maud had known her in Boston, and it was a mutual pleasure to meet again here. If there is anything that draws friendship and acquaintance into closer ties it is to meet in a foreign land. Not long after her arrival she came into their parlor, where the two girls were seated by themselves. Maud had been teasing Edyth, and, as soon as the customary greetings were exchanged, said to Mrs. Arlington that they had been philosophizing on love, and asked her to give them her ideas of that grand passion.

A shadow passed over the beautiful widow's face as she thought on her fast-receding youth, and the dreams of a vanished ideal rose up before her vision as she reflected on the might-have-been.

"Girls," she said, in a solemn tone, "that is no theme upon which to narrate an idle tale. It is the one great mainspring of the human race. For aught I know, it may descend to animals as well as man, and perhaps to inanimate nature and to the mineral and vegetable worlds. In my early youth, in the spring-time of my life, I laughed at love. In my midsummertime I have cried at love. When I reach the winter of my life, and finally descend to the grave, I hope to be sustained by a heavenly love Go to the forest shade, and there you will see the cooing dove, a simile fit for a poet's pen to adorn this theme. The wild waste of waters is filled with its many finny inhabitants, who yearly ascend the neighboring streams in their annual pilgrimage of love. Across the desert's sands are borne the seeds of trees, which, meeting in their path a proper seed, will reunite and reproduce their kind. This may be love. When I was young it was our custom to spend the summer days upon the sea-beat shore. Night after night I looked across the flowing tide and saw the beacon light, way out at sea, throwing its warning rays upon the treacherous shoals. An answering light, near by the coast, took up the task, and spread its protecting

rays upon the rocks, and so on down
the shore. Upon those waves it was
my delight to roam. My sister and
myself oft rowed far out to sea, and
there we laid upon the ocean's heart
and dreamed of fate. It was there I
met my first youthful love. Although
an interval of many years has passed
since then, yet even now I can look
back across the lapse of time and see
in fancy that loved form. Full fifteen
years have passed since last we met;
nor do I know if the pure air of heaven
now gives him life, or whether the dark
and pestilential charnel-house forever
closes over what was his; and I have
been another's bride; yet this I'll say—
that if he is yet alive, and once again
desired that I be his, I would exchange
all that I have and follow him throughout the world. I tell you, girls, that
Heaven frowns down upon an ill-as-
sorted love; and now, while you have
still the choice, let your selection be one

such that you can love. Do not allow
an idle word, or the estrangement of
a passing hour, to mar your future
for all coming time. Such fate was
mine. It was just at one of these
crises of my life, when one word alone,
even one gesture, would have changed
my after life, wherein I failed. The
lover of my youth had poured impassioned language in my ears, and
strove by eloquence alone to move
my heart. He then was poor. His
future was before him, and he had first
to win his way with men before he
could claim me. He asked me would
I wait. I see it now, as if the scene
were only yesterday, and but a single
night had intervened, instead of fifteen
years and death. The important hour
came amidst a brilliant scene, and in
a hall well filled with men and women
in their gay attire. It was at a ball.
I carried in my hand a floral offering
from a wealthy friend, and made great

ostentation of that empty gift. He
told me that the next day's sun must
see him on his way to seek his fortune;
that an unexpected opening had been
laid before him, and he must go. I
laughed. In solemn earnest he laid
down the alternative before me. He
said: 'I only ask you to delay your
answer to all other suitors until I
have had the opportunity of hewing
out my way. You know I am poor,
but, armed with your assurance that
if I won both wealth and fame, your
love would crown my efforts with your
hand, I would start out in life with
the certainty of winning. I know I
have already won your heart; I must
have time before I win your hand!'
Again I laughed. He heeded not the
interruption, but went on. 'You see
the hands of yonder clock, slow eking
out the lapse of time? I will wait
until the two unite in one and mark
the period of twelve. If by that time

you should decide to answer yes, take
out that pure white rose from its companion flowers, and place it in your
bosom; but if fate has it in store for
me that you answer no, then let it
rest. I cannot bear the pain of being
near you at our parting hour with
others looking on. Answer yes, and
I will find a way to see you once again
before I go; but if you answer no, I
will not inflict my pain upon you, but
pass from out your life without a
further word!' He kept his promise.
He held aloof while others pressed
around me, and it seemed as if my
spirits were so high that they would
carry me away before I curbed them.
Once I caught a sight of his sad face.
Its image was so impressed upon my
vision that I can recall it now at will.
As the hour approached I took a seat
far from the crowd. He moved so as
he could see me. When the first stroke
of the cathedral gong sounded upon

the whirling scene I took the flower
out from its hold, and plucked the
leaves from off the parent stem. His
gaze met mine, and what felt like a
penetrating ray appeared to reach
from him to me. When the last stroke
had sounded out the final count I
dropped the plucked leaves upon the
floor and crushed them with my foot,
then sought his gaze; but he was
gone. From that hour to this I have
never seen him, nor have I ever yet received another token. That was love."

A silence fell upon the group. Mrs.
Arlington had spoken from her heart.
It had been a relief to her to pour out
the pent-up feelings of so many years
to these sympathetic listeners. At
length she resumed:

"I do not know why to-night I
have been impelled to resurrect the
past, and lay the inner history of my
life before you. But let that go.
What has once been said can never be

unsaid, and I will not sadden such a
merry lot as yours by woes of mine."

With that she somewhat hastily
left, for her emotions had been great,
and she now preferred to conceal all
further feeling.

Hardly had she gone ere Colonel
Carter appeared upon the scene, and
bade them good-evening. It was a
pleasant sight to Maud to witness
the first meeting between him and
Edyth. He advanced with such a
light and eager footstep, while she
received him with slow-moving action
and downcast eyes. But Maud was
irrepressible. She had become very
fond of Colonel Carter in that way
that two persons of similar tastes are
drawn together. She had in vain
tried to tease him, after a manner
which would have set Edyth perfectly
wild, but which he parried so skilfully as to lose all its force. Whenever she was in the parlor when he

called she remained just long enough
for him to begin to wish her away;
then she would start off at a frantic
speed on some perfectly trivial errand,
at the same time making elaborate
and unnecessary excuses for being
compelled to leave him alone with
Edyth. As soon as Colonel Carter
was seated she began chaffing him,
in expectation of throwing him into
confusion by the suddenness of her
attack.

"Colonel," she said, while a mischievous twinkle in her eyes warned
him of what was coming, "we have
just been discussing 'what is love,'
and a friend of ours from Boston has
given us a description of her idea,
which was so lugubrious that it put
Edyth and myself in the dumps.
Won't you give us your idea, so that
we may profit by it?" and with this
she merrily laughed at the absurdity
of Colonel Carter's trying to give to

them together what he had reserved
for Edyth's ear alone.

"Ah, Miss Maud," he replied,
without being disconcerted in the
least, "you are always giving me a
heavy task to do; but I will enter
into an agreement with you that if
you will tell me 'what *is* love,' I will
tell you 'what love *was*.'"

"Agreed," cried Maud, "and
should you come to any episode
which in its nature is too much for
my inexperienced youth, I will shut
my eyes and stop up my ears, and
thus be blind and deaf"; for she had
heard of the tiger and the drive, and
had long wanted the opportunity of
teasing him.

"But you must begin first," he
playfully rejoined, as he entered into
the spirit of the thing. Moreover he
desired to see what the effect of all
this would be upon Edyth, who was
sitting very quietly by her cousin, but

evidently getting nervous over the
turn that the conversation had taken.

"What do I call love?" the merry
girl inquired, as a reminiscence of a
mischievous something flitted across
her memory, and an experience in her
own life came back with full force
upon her; for she, too, had stirred up
the grand passion in a man. She had
met him at one of those innumerable
charitable entertainments of which
she was the leading spirit, and her
vivacious manners had captured him
by storm. He wore spectacles, and
was always stumbling over something, and looked as if he needed a
nurse; so, when in an opportune moment he had asked her to be his guardian angel through life, she had utterly
disconcerted him by a peal of laughter.
At the same time she muttered to herself, after the manner of her Latin
exercises, guardian angel—*videlicet*,
wearer of the pantaloon. Her domine,

as she facetiously nicknamed him, never had the courage to approach her again. It was sometimes an amusement for her to see him furtively glance out of the sides of his spectacles as she came in his neighborhood; but he beat such precipitate retreats that she never could overtake him. Soon their paths in life drifted apart, and the leaf was turned down over her first love-scene.

"What do I call love?" she asked again. "It is the essence of the concentrated extract of the human heart. It begins with the child at its birth; it ends with old age at the grave. You will see the youngest school-boy laden with the books of his little sweetheart. Tottering along under his extra load, he is the incarnation of an early love. Grown older, he is too shy to talk, but sits afar off and speaks with his eyes. Sometimes he builds an edifice of mud, which his

9

vivid imagination transforms into a dwelling, and which he fills with his imaginings. Again, grown older, his youthful ardor tinges his dreams with images of houris. His fancy dwells upon the East, and he luxuriates in the harem's smiles. A man, and visions of a home, made sweetly welcome from a wife and child, rise up before him. But the fond devotion of a woman's love cannot find attribute in words. Language cannot express the subtle influence that is there. The Tartar maiden mounts her steed and flees, and calls that love. The Indian virgin sits and smiles, and is exchanged for so much barter. She thinks that's love. It lurks in palaces and stately halls. It builds the cottage and the robin's nest. It's found around the fireside. It dwells amidst the flowers. It forms a prize for which men often strive in arms. Again, it hovers over their recreation and their games. I've known the royal game to hide young love."

She spoke with a comic serious-ness and with a swing like that of a school-boy repeating an early lesson in elocution. Her parody was per-fect. Hers was somewhat akin to bright Mercutio's style when that witty gallant laughed at love. The last sentence was a heavy hit at the Colonel and Edyth; but he parried it with a good-humored remark.

"Now, Colonel," she demanded, "it is your turn to tell us what is love."

He paused a little. A shadow passed over his countenance, which just before had been lighted up with amusement at her clever recital. He was contrasting his present feeling towards the fair young girl—whose heart he knew he had now won, and whose hand he expected to claim

when the autumn leaves would begin
to fall—with the fiery passion of his
earlier youth. He had long thought
that he would tell her of it; that he
would candidly confess to her that he
had loved before, and lay open his
whole life to her, so that there should
be no secrets between them. That
there should be absolute confidence
between them he knew would be the
one eternal bulwark of their love.
But he had not courage to do it yet.
When he was alone with her, time
was too precious to be wasted on the
past; the present was to be enjoyed
to the utmost. He clothed his language in allegory, but he told her thus
of his early love, little dreaming that
she had heard it just before:

"You ask me what is love. I will
reply by telling what love was. Many
years ago, when the dark cloud of
war had burst upon this land, and,
having spread destruction before it,

had ended with the calm that succeeds
a storm, a young man found himself
on his father's fields, with enough
saved to start again in life on the
road to fortune. He collected all the
produce and the materials of the
farm into one building and adjoining
lot, so as to be ready then for ship-
ment to the foreign trade. But the
wild passions lately stirred by war
found far greater evils in the so-called
peace. A host of wicked scoundrels
came upon the land, worse than any
form of war, since they were cowards,
and did in darkness their foul deeds.
One such found credence with the idle
blacks, and put such vicious ideas in
their ignorant minds that they followed him like sheep and did his bidding. He told them that these savings all were theirs, and that all they
had to do was just to wait until the
night brought covering to their deeds,
when they could take all—the theft to

be concealed by burning the barn.
They did it. One slight stroke of the
match, and in an instant the accumulated wealth of years was wrapped
in flames. What wonder is it that
when this foul deed was done my
hero was forced to seek in other
climes the road to fortune. He left
his native land for many years, but
when at last he had enriched himself
he returned, and with his means
and skill aided his country's progress.
Meanwhile he passed through many
vicissitudes of place and things. His
path in life once led him to the ocean's
side. There he had met two sisters,
in their early youth great rovers on
its wave. When youth and beauty
come in contact with an ardent soul,
it is but nature that they think as
one. He loved. Far out at sea he
sent his signal light, which, answering
with her parlor lamp, made meeting
certain. When angry winter, close

following on the summer's joys, drove
them to shelter in the city's hills, they
met again. His open-sesame of lineage made him welcome at the feast,
and for skilled and easy motion he
was sought for in the dance. They
often met abroad. At home he sometimes sought her, but there his presence was not welcomed by its inmates,
since a wealthier suitor was preferred.
At last an opening came for him in
life, but it required that he should go
and hunt in other regions for its
wealth. He sought her out to tell
her of his gain; that he must go, and
ask her that she wait. He found her
midst a brilliant scene, in gay attire,
enjoying time in measures of the
mazy dance. She carried in her hand
some flowers, whose perfumed rich-
ness she inhaled quite often, though
those flowers, when marked by contrast with her damask cheek, were
put to shame. He told her that his

hour had come; that he must go,
and she must say that night the word
whose promise would urge him on to
win his recompense from her, or end his
woe (for love is often woe).   The time
was inauspicious, for the whirl and
rush of many dancers shared the time
wherein he could plead with her.   He
told her when the dial hand struck
twelve upon a clock which near by
measured out the time alike to grave
and gay, she must decide.   If for him,
then she must take a flower and place
it in her bosom; but if not, she was to
omit that sign.   Time crept along.   At
last the minute hand approached the
sign which marks high noon or else
the hour when evil spirits leave their
homes and wander o'er the land.   As
the hour drew near she took from its
companions a sweet rose.   Now had
the moment of decision come.   His
blood coursed rapid through his
veins.   His breath came fast.   His

nerves were strung up to their highest
pitch. He once had stood as steady
as the rock itself by Stonewall Jackson's side. He oft had faced the
leaden messenger of death, and had
not quailed. He had led a troop of men
far up a hillside slope whose crest was
serried with the cannons' mouths,
and had not feared. But now, before
this fair young girl, whose frame he
could have crushed with his stout
hand, he trembled and grew pale.
That was love. The hammer's stroke
fell on the silent gong, and one sound
came out from its pent-up home. She
plucked a leaf off from the parent
stem, and listened. Again a tone,
that seemed to execrate the hammer's
blow, came ringing round the room.
She plucked some other leaves, then
listened. A harsh and broken noise
now ushered in the third alarm.
Again she stripped the blooming
flower of some fair leaves, then
waited for the gong. In his native

village he had heard the church-bell
mark the flight of time. Its notes
had echoed through the fields, and
had come as music when the day's
work was done. In the morn it called
to energy and life from unsubstantial
dreams. Therefore he had learned to
love the music of that church-like
tone. But the sound that now beat,
clamoring in his ears, changed into
discord those fond dreams. From
that hour he never could endure those
sweet cathedral tones. When the
last stroke had finished she threw
down the unoffending leaves and
crushed them with her foot. Joy-
bearing-hope faded away at the fall
of the flowers, and love fled at the
death of hope."

As it gradually became apparent
that the tales of Colonel Carter and
Mrs. Arlington were the same, Maud
concluded that it was time for her to
go; that it would never do for her to
remain any longer, and she had quietly

arisen, and was going on tiptoe from the room as he ceased speaking.

After he had paused a moment, he leaned over, and, in a tone so low that she alone could hear, said to Edyth: "Darling, what do you call love?"

The question was very sudden; the emotions she had experienced when Mrs. Arlington told her tale were those of deepest sympathy. She was alternately pleased and dismayed at Maud's delineation; but when the only man she had ever loved told her thus of his love for another, and that, too, for one who had just confessed an eternal fealty towards himself, she was overcome. The blood surged to her heart, and when he called her for the first time by a name she had sometimes only dared to whisper to herself, it was too much. Her senses reeled. As her cousin, thoroughly alarmed, bent over her prostrate form, she whispered, "this is love."

CHAPTER IX.

THE DEATH OF LOVE.

The gaiety at the Huguenot was at its height. Balls and theatricals were on the tapis, and innumerable drives and excursions on the river were being planned. The dam at Maiden's Adventure, where the legend had it that her lover's life was saved by a young girl swimming the river and giving him timely warning, was most popular with those romantically inclined. Its broad sheet, extending far up the river, gave abundant opportunity for imagination to line its shores with fancied creations. The rocks overhanging the river were well adapted for the artist's brush, and the wide expanse of water furnished a field for the sportsman's skill.

As Colonel Carter was preparing the next evening to attend one of the full-dress balls, he was taken by surprise by his brother coming in somewhat excitedly and exclaiming, "They've done it, they've done it; these waters have done it." When asked to explain what had been done, he took no notice of the question, but paraded up and down the room, now and then scanning his reflection in the looking-glass. Randolph Carter looked at his brother in silent amazement, which was intensified by his immediate question.

"Ran.," he said, "now, putting all joking aside, don't you think I've spruced up wonderfully in the last few days, and have gotten to be a good-looking fellow?"

A horrible suspicion began to take hold of Randolph, that Peyton might

have gone crazy. Before he had time
to frame a suitable reply Peyton continued:

"You know, Ran., you advised me
to drink a barrel full of these waters.
Well, I went at it systematically, and
I believe I have so far gotten through
with half a one. It has done me a
world of good. I feel as if I was
fully equal to these young whipper-
snappers, that can dance all night
and not mind it the next day; and
I'll tell you, Ran., this rejuvenation
has enabled me to capture a young
and handsome widow who has just
arrived at the hotel."

Randolph Carter was in a dilemma.
His brother's antics were so strange,
and his language so excited, that he
felt sure that some untoward accident
had thrown his reason from its bal-
ance, and that he was not himself.
He had heard that the best way was
to humor persons in this condition,

therefore he said: "Tell me all about it, old fellow."

His brother assumed a more rational tone and said: "You see, Ran., I was coming through the long corridor of the hotel, near the ladies' parlor, just about dusk, when I met the handsome widow. She had been pointed out to me, so that I knew her by sight, and I was casting about in my mind how to get an early introduction to her, so as to have an anchor to windward, as these yachting fellows say, the aforesaid windward being the host of young duffers that always hang around a rich woman, when, judge of my surprise as she held out her hand and said, 'Mr. Carter, is it possible that we have met again, in this remote region, after so many years of separation?' Now you know, Ran., I always keep an eye on the coast to see that it is clear; well I was pretty sure that nobody was about, and besides it was a little dark, so, when I took her hand it was so soft and small that I could not help kissing it. I would never have had the assurance to have done this, had it not been for that half-barrel. I expected to have received a severe overhauling, but I was feeling my oats and was ready for it. Well, sir, instead of giving me Jesse, she blushed crimson and said, 'you have not, then, forgotten the past?' Now, I have often thought that in my early youth I might have whispered soft nothings into a willing ear; and afterwards, to my shame be it said, have forgotten all about it, and although, to save my neck, I could not recollect where I had met this Dulcinea before, yet I did something very much like what a trooper is supposed to do. I told her that it was best that the past should be forgotten, but that she herself could never be forgot. I must have made a lucky hit. She replied that the past must be forgiven in order to be forgot. I still retained her hand, which I thought it opportune to squeeze. She gently released it. She told me that she had a yacht anchored in the river, and asked me would I take a cruise with her and her duenna. Barkis was very willing, and we go on board to-night, so as to take the early morning tide. In fact, the train leaves in half an hour, so I must be getting ready."

This lengthy explanation relieved Randolph's mind from apprehension of his brother's sanity, but it was rather strange.

"What did you say was the name of your inamorata?" he asked, as he tried to reconcile the phenomenon of Peyton's rapid success with the usual dilatory proceedings in such cases.

"I did not mention the name,"

Peyton replied, "but she is a Mrs. Arlington, from Boston."

A glimmering of the truth flashed across his mind.

"Do you know her name before her marriage, or can you describe her appearance?" Randolph queried.

"I might as well attempt to paint the Sistine Madonna or sing the Last Farewell as to endeavor to do justice to her appearance by a description," Peyton enthusiastically replied. "Her maiden name was Stanley, Irene Stanley!"

That name, which he had not dared to breathe for many years, for fear it might awake a slumbering passion from its buried hold, was spoken to him unconcernedly by his brother. He had thought its mention would unloose a wild and frenzied longing, but the name had lost its magic power. The flame which once had burned with such consuming heat had now died out and left but ashes. Man can put out the light, but who can start the vital flame again?

As soon as his brother mentioned the name, Randolph Carter perceived that his surmise was correct; that this indeed was his early love, and that accident had once more brought their paths together. He now understood how it was that she had taken his brother for himself, and was under a delusion. Should he speak, or, by keeping silent, allow the error to go on?

"Peyton," he finally said, "you are playing a dangerous game; your fond Dulcinea has probably taken you for some one else, and will soon unmask you. However, there is no reason why you should not go; but do not deceive her in any manner, shape or form. Should she allude to the 'dead past,' you answer with the 'living present.' Now, fare you well."

The brothers parted with high hopes and dreams. They little realized what a heavy blow fate had in keeping for one of them, and under what trying circumstances they would meet again.

While this conversation was taking place between the brothers, a somewhat similar one was taking place between two *attaches* of the hotel, and which Edyth accidentally overheard. She, too, was about to get ready for the ball, and had left their parlor for that purpose, leaving the door, which connected her room with it, somewhat ajar. The colored servant-girl came in to rekindle the fire, when a fellow-servant followed her in, and soliloquized somewhat as follows:

"'Fore de Lor! Lucindy, don't talk 'bout de white folks and de colored ladies. I'se seed a little while go a white lady carry on shameful.

Why, I'd had mor' mods'ty dan dat mysef. It war like dis. Dat ar white lady dat am got a boat down yonder in de ribber—dey calls it sum hifiluting name, but it am no mor' dan a boat—she comes out of de parlor jest 'bout same time Culn. Carter, he comes along de flor. Culn. Carter, he am a mighty likely gemmun, dow my flowman, Pete, sez he do drink dese here sulfur waters mor' dan any pusson he eber did see. I spose dat what mak him so frisky. Well, he cums 'long, as I sez, jest as de white lady cums out. Wal, what you spose she do? She put out her hand jest like dis, and sez sumthing 'bout 'cognizin' him, and forgiben, an all dat ar trash. Culn. Carter no mor' idee who she war dan a man in de moon; but de ole sinner, don't you bliebe he had de imperence nuf to shake hans, and den he smacked it, den kept hold ob it. I don't blame de Culn. much, for eny

man dat am eny count will buck up to
a gal if she let him; but dat ar white
lady jest gib him all de chance he
want. She ax him to go wid hur on
dat boat, and go a sumthing I dunno
much 'bout; sumthing like bruzing.
She tell him he muss go rite off, to tek
a mornin' ride, and I jest now seed
dem go down to de train dat goes to
Richmond dis ebening. Dat ar white
lady was gwine to stay here sum time,
but after she cotched de Culn. she hus-
sle him rite 'bout. I calls dat a fur-
rard thing in hur. How kin dey spose
de cullud lady gwine do diffrent
when de white lady carries on like
dat?"

Edyth by this time had grown
sufficiently familiar with the negro
dialect to understand. She stood
spell-bound as she listened. She had
not yet met Peyton Carter, nor did
she know of his arrival. The coinci-
dence of the two accounts of their

early loves left no doubt in her mind
but that the old love had prevailed,
and that she had been abandoned.
Oh, how she had been mistaken in
this man! He had appeared to her
all that was noble and generous and
good. She had thrilled with pride
whenever the success which he had
won had been brought before her.
She had entered thoroughly into his
aims and ambition in life, and shared
them with him. Oh, how well he
filled that aching void which her helpless womanhood had created, by her
desire to share in the world's great
progress. Must she descend to the
ignoble routine of her former life, and
end her days in commonplace beati-
tudes? And he was gone, already
gone, without one word of warning
or a last farewell! It was better so;
the one sharp cut of the knife, the
sudden wrench, is better than a drawn-
out pain. She would forgive, but she

could ne'er forget. It was no fault
of hers that in an era when she was
yet a child he should have loved; that
in the spring-time of her life she should
be spurned—that struck a seething-
iron in her soul. But let him go.
She'd not condemn him till she heard
him tell what he might have to say
why he should not forfeit all esteem
and love. Should he never have the
strength to tell his weakness it might
go untold. But let him go. The
world should never see that she had
cared. She would be gay and smile,
so they would not know. To-night
she'd revel in the dance, and suffer
with the sun. When she had braved
it all she would retire, and none
should know. Had she the strength
to do it? If hers failed, there was
the artificial stimulant whose taste
would aid her to it. When it was
done she'd leave this spot, so hallowed
yet so sad. But to-night; there was

the rub. As yet she was arrayed but scantily. She would put on such raiment as would become her best, then join the throng.

A sudden inhalation seemed to lift the load from off her spirits. A quickened step, which she had learned to tell, a voice whose every flection she now knew so well, her ear arrested. Could it be that memory had evoked an echo from its cave to haunt her with its presence! Again that voice; this time distinct and true. "Tell her I'll wait in here." The card, the voice, the name, the unseen presence in the neighboring room—all proved that he was there. She paused to gather thought, to feel that this was real, and to keep still the wild tumult in her heart and soul. Time passed unheeded till the tiny bell chimed from her clock the quarter hour that he had waited. She must delay no longer. Hastily donning her other raiment,

and hurriedly fastening it, she entered.
Wearied with waiting, her lover had
reclined his head upon his hand, and
was reposing in the arms of sleep.
She walked on tiptoe till she stood
beside him, then a wild and sudden
longing to gently touch his forehead
with her lips, as plea for pardon for
the wrong she just now did him, took
strong hold upon her.   She had
stooped to carry out this inspiration
when a soft and radiant smile over-
spread his countenance.   He awoke.

"Light of my soul," he cried, "do
you indeed stand thus before me, or
has some unsubstantial emanation
from my brain evoked your image so
to mock me?"

This impassioned language somewhat startled her, and she drew back.
Hastily springing up, he took her
hand to prevent all further separation, and continued: "Do not leave
me, or thus draw away, as if our

contact was as that of a loathsome something or the contamination of a death-darting cockatrice."

Again she somewhat drew away to slightly soften his increasing fervor. He gently put his arm around her waist and held her firmly, though she resisted this. Her dress became entangled in his sleeve and her struggle broke its fastening from around her throat. Quick as a lightning flash he stooped and kissed her; there where the tender nerves are concentrated in their greatest strength his lips just touched her. The life-blood, throbbing with its greatest force, received an impulse which extended to the heart. The accumulated strain broke down its valves and pulsation ceased.

Her spirit fled up to its starry home. The Great Creator received into His fold once more the living soul, and the King of Terrors claimed the extinct form, for love to her was death.

CPSIA information can be obtained
at www.ICGtesting.com
Printed in the USA
BVHW090045030122
625213BV00008B/704